THE
HATED SON

HONORE DE BALZAC

Translated By Katharine Prescott Wormeley

1st WORLD
LIBRARY
Literary Society

The Hated Son

Honore de Balzac

© 1st World Library, 2006
PO Box 2211
Fairfield, IA 52556
www.1stworldlibrary.com
First Edition

LCCN: 2006907707

Softcover ISBN: 1-4218-2428-0
Hardcover ISBN: 1-4218-2328-4
eBook ISBN: 1-4218-2528-7

Purchase *"The Hated Son"*
as a traditional bound book at:
www.1stWorldLibrary.com/purchase.asp?ISBN=1-4218-2428-0

1st World Library is a literary, educational organization
dedicated to:

- Creating a free internet library of downloadable ebooks

- Hosting writing competitions and offering book
publishing scholarships.

Interested in more 1st World Library books?
contact: literacy@1stworldlibrary.com

Check us out at: www.1stworldlibrary.com

1st World Library Literary Society

Giving Back to the World

"If you want to work on the core problem, it's early school literacy."

- James Barksdale, former CEO of Netscape

"No skill is more crucial to the future of a child, or to a democratic and prosperous society, than literacy."

- Los Angeles Times

Literacy... means far more than learning how to read and write... The aim is to transmit... knowledge and promote social participation."

- UNESCO

"Literacy is not a luxury, it is a right and a responsibility. If our world is to meet the challenges of the twenty-first century we must harness the energy and creativity of all our citizens."

- President Bill Clinton

"Parents should be encouraged to read to their children, and teachers should be equipped with all available techniques for teaching literacy, so the varying needs and capacities of individual kids can be taken into account."

- Hugh Mackay

DEDICATION

To Madame la Baronne James Rothschild.

PART I

HOW THE MOTHER LIVED

CHAPTER I

A BEDROOM OF THE SIXTEENTH CENTURY

On a winter's night, about two in the morning, the Comtesse Jeanne d'Herouville felt such violent pains that in spite of her inexperience, she was conscious of an approaching confinement; and the instinct which makes us hope for ease in a change of posture induced her to sit up in her bed, either to study the nature of these new sufferings, or to reflect on her situation. She was a prey to cruel fears, - caused less by the dread of a first lying-in, which terrifies most women, than by certain dangers which awaited her child.

In order not to awaken her husband who was sleeping beside her, the poor woman moved with precautions which her intense terror made as minute as those of a prisoner endeavoring to escape. Though the pains became more and more severe, she ceased to feel them, so completely did she concentrate her own strength on the painful effort of resting her two moist hands on the pillow and so turning her suffering body from a posture in which she could find no ease. At the slightest rustling of the huge green silk coverlet, under which she had slept but little since her marriage, she stopped as though she had rung a bell. Forced to watch the count, she divided her attention between the folds of the rustling stuff and a large swarthy face, the moustache of which was brushing her shoulder. When some noisier breath than usual left her husband's lips, she was filled with a sudden terror that revived the color driven from her cheeks by her double anguish.

The prisoner reached the prison door in the dead of night and trying to noiselessly turn the key in a pitiless lock, was never more timidly bold.

When the countess had succeeded in rising to her seat without awakening her keeper, she made a gesture of childlike joy which revealed the touching naivete of her nature. But the half-formed smile on her burning lips was quickly suppressed; a thought came to darken that pure brow, and her long blue eyes resumed their sad expression. She gave a sigh and again laid her hands, not without precaution, on the fatal conjugal pillow. Then - as if for the first time since her marriage she found herself free in thought and action - she looked at the things around her, stretching out her neck with little darting motions like those of a bird in its cage. Seeing her thus, it was easy to divine that she had once been all gaiety and light-heartedness, but that fate had suddenly mown down her hopes, and changed her ingenuous gaiety to sadness.

The chamber was one of those which, to this day octogenarian porters of old chateaus point out to visitors as "the state bedroom where Louis XIII. once slept." Fine pictures, mostly brown in tone, were framed in walnut, the delicate carvings of which were blackened by time. The rafters of the ceiling formed

Honore de Balzac

compartments adorned with arabesques in the style of the preceding century, which preserved the colors of the chestnut wood. These decorations, severe in tone, reflected the light so little that it was difficult to see their designs, even when the sun shone full into that long and wide and lofty chamber. The silver lamp, placed upon the mantel of the vast fireplace, lighted the room so feebly that its quivering gleam could be compared only to the nebulous stars which appear at moments through the dun gray clouds of an autumn night. The fantastic figures crowded on the marble of the fireplace, which was opposite to the bed, were so grotesquely hideous that she dared not fix her eyes upon them, fearing to see them move, or to hear a startling laugh from their gaping and twisted mouths.

At this moment a tempest was growling in the chimney, giving to every puff of wind a lugubrious meaning, - the vast size of the flute putting the hearth into such close communication with the skies above that the embers upon it had a sort of respiration; they sparkled and went out at the will of the wind. The arms of the family of Herouville, carved in white marble with their mantle and supporters, gave the appearance of a tomb to this species of edifice, which formed a pendant to the bed, another erection raised to the glory of Hymen. Modern architects would have been puzzled to decide whether the room had been built for the bed or the bed for the room. Two cupids playing on the walnut headboard, wreathed with garlands, might have passed for angels; and columns of the same wood, supporting the tester were carved with mythological allegories, the explanation of which could have been found either in the Bible or Ovid's Metamorphoses. Take away the bed, and the same tester would have served in a church for the canopy of the pulpit or the seats of the wardens. The married pair mounted by three steps to this sumptuous couch, which stood upon a platform and was hung with curtains of green silk covered with brilliant designs called "ramages" - possibly because the birds of gay plumage there depicted were supposed to sing. The folds of these immense curtains were so stiff that in the semi-darkness they might have been taken for some metal fabric. On the green velvet hanging, adorned with gold fringes, which covered the foot of this lordly couch the superstition of the Comtes d'Herouville had affixed a large crucifix, on which their chaplain placed a fresh branch of sacred box when he renewed at Easter the holy water in the basin at the foot of the cross.

On one side of the fireplace stood a large box or wardrobe of choice woods magnificently carved, such as brides receive even now in the provinces on their wedding day. These old chests, now so much in request by antiquaries, were the arsenals from which women drew the rich and elegant treasures of their personal adornment, - laces, bodices, high collars and ruffs, gowns of price, alms-purses, masks, gloves, veils, - in fact all the inventions of coquetry in the sixteenth century.

On the other side, by way of symmetry, was another piece of furniture, somewhat similar in shape, where the countess kept her books, papers, and jewels. Antique chairs covered with damask, a large and greenish mirror, made in Venice, and richly framed in a sort of rolling toilet-table, completed the furnishings of the room. The floor was covered with a Persian carpet, the richness of which proved the gallantry of the count; on the upper step of the bed stood a little table, on which the waiting-woman served every night in a gold or silver cup a drink prepared with spices.

After we have gone some way in life we know the secret influence exerted by places on the condition of the soul. Who has not had his darksome moments, when fresh hope has come into his heart from things that surrounded him? The fortunate, or the unfortunate man, attributes an intelligent countenance to the things among which he lives; he listens to them, he consults them - so naturally superstitious is he. At this moment the countess turned her eyes upon all these articles of furniture, as if they were living beings whose help and protection she implored; but the answer of that sombre luxury seemed to her inexorable.

Suddenly the tempest redoubled. The poor young woman could augur nothing favorable as she listened to the threatening heavens, the changes of which were interpreted in those credulous days according to the ideas or the habits of individuals. Suddenly she turned her eyes to the two arched windows at the end of the room; but the smallness of their panes and the multiplicity of the leaden lines did not allow her to see the sky and judge if the world were coming to an end, as certain monks, eager for donations, affirmed. She might easily have believed in such predictions, for the noise of the angry sea, the waves of which beat against the castle wall, combined with the mighty voice of the tempest, so that even the rocks appeared to shake. Though her sufferings were now becoming keener and less endurable, the countess dared not awaken her husband; but she turned and examined his features, as if despair were urging her to find a consolation there against so many sinister forebodings.

If matters were sad around the poor young woman, that

face, notwithstanding the tranquillity of sleep, seemed sadder still. The light from the lamp, flickering in the draught, scarcely reached beyond the foot of the bed and illumined the count's head capriciously; so that the fitful movements of its flash upon those features in repose produced the effect of a struggle with angry thought. The countess was scarcely reassured by perceiving the cause of that phenomenon. Each time that a gust of wind projected the light upon the count's large face, casting shadows among its bony outlines, she fancied that her husband was about to fix upon her his two insupportably stern eyes.

Implacable as the war then going on between the Church and Calvinism, the count's forehead was threatening even while he slept. Many furrows, produced by the emotions of a warrior life, gave it a vague resemblance to the vermiculated stone which we see in the buildings of that period; his hair, like the whitish lichen of old oaks, gray before its time, surrounded without grace a cruel brow, where religious intolerance showed its passionate brutality. The shape of the aquiline nose, which resembled the beak of a bird of prey, the black and crinkled lids of the yellow eyes, the prominent bones of a hollow face, the rigidity of the wrinkles, the disdain expressed in the lower lip, were all expressive of ambition, despotism, and power, the more to be feared because the narrowness of the skull betrayed an almost total absence of intelligence, and a mere brute courage devoid of generosity. The face was horribly disfigured by a large transversal scar which had the appearance of a second mouth on the right cheek.

At the age of thirty-three the count, anxious to distinguish himself in that unhappy religious war the signal for which was given on Saint-Bartholomew's day, had been grievously wounded at the siege of Rochelle. The misfortune of this wound increased his hatred against the partisans of what the language of that day called "the Religion," but, by a not unnatural turn of mind, he included in that antipathy all handsome men. Before the catastrophe, however, he was so repulsively ugly that no lady had ever been willing to receive him as a suitor. The only passion of his youth was for a celebrated woman called La Belle Romaine. The distrust resulting from this new misfortune made him suspicious to the point of not believing himself capable of inspiring a true passion; and his character became so savage that when he did have some successes in gallantry he owed them to the terror inspired by his cruelty. The left hand of this terrible Catholic, which lay on the outside of the bed, will complete this sketch of his character. Stretched out as if to guard the countess, as a miser guards his hoard, that enormous hand was covered with hair so thick, it presented such a network of veins and projecting muscles, that it gave the idea of a branch of birch clasped with a growth of yellowing ivy.

Children looking at the count's face would have thought him an ogre, terrible tales of whom they knew by heart. It was enough to see the width and length of the space occupied by the count in the bed, to imagine his gigantic proportions. When awake, his gray eyebrows hid his eyelids in a way to heighten the light of his eye, which glittered with the luminous ferocity of a wolf skulking on the watch in a forest. Under his lion nose, with its flaring nostrils, a large and ill-kept moustache (for he despised all toilet niceties) completely concealed the upper lip. Happily for the countess, her husband's wide mouth was silent at this moment, for the softest sounds of that harsh voice made her tremble. Though the Comte d'Herouville was barely fifty years of age, he appeared at first sight to be sixty, so much had the toils of war, without injuring his robust constitution, dilapidated him physically.

The countess, who was now in her nineteenth year, made a painful contrast to that large, repulsive figure. She was fair and slim. Her chestnut locks, threaded with gold, played upon her neck like russet shadows, and defined a face such as Carlo Dolce has painted for his ivory-toned madonnas, - a face which now seemed ready to expire under the increasing attacks of physical pain. You might have thought her the apparition of an angel sent from heaven to soften the iron will of the terrible count.

"No, he will not kill us!" she cried to herself mentally, after contemplating her husband for a long time. "He is frank, courageous, faithful to his word - faithful to his word!"

Repeating that last sentence in her thoughts, she trembled violently, and remained as if stupefied.

To understand the horror of her present situation, we must add that this nocturnal scene took place in 1591, a period when civil war raged throughout France, and the laws had no vigor. The excesses of the League, opposed to the accession of Henri IV., surpassed the calamities of the religious wars. License was so universal that no one was surprised to see a great lord kill his enemy in open day. When a military expedition, having a private object, was led in the name of the King or of the League, one or other of these parties applauded it. It was thus that Blagny, a soldier, came near becoming a sovereign prince at the gates of France. Sometime before Henri III.'s death, a court lady murdered a nobleman who made offensive remarks about her. One of the king's minions remarked to him: -

"Hey! vive Dieu! sire, she daggered him finely!"

The Comte d'Herouville, one of the most rabid royalists in Normandy, kept the part of that province which adjoins Brittany under subjection to Henri IV. by the rigor of his executions. The head of one of the richest families in France, he had considerably increased the revenues of his great estates by marrying seven months before the night on which this history begins, Jeanne de Saint-Savin, a young lady who, by a not uncommon chance in days when people were killed off like flies, had suddenly become the representative of both branches of the Saint-Savin family. Necessity and terror were the causes which led to this union. At a banquet given, two months after the marriage, to the Comte and Comtesse d'Herouville, a discussion arose on a topic which in those days of ignorance was thought amusing: namely, the legitimacy of children coming into the world ten months after the death of their fathers, or seven months after the wedding day.

"Madame," said the count brutally, turning to his wife, "if you give me a child ten months after my death, I cannot help it; but be careful that you are not brought to bed in seven months!"

"What would you do then, old bear?" asked the young Marquis de Verneuil, thinking that the count was joking.

"I should wring the necks of mother and child!"

An answer so peremptory closed the discussion, imprudently started by a seigneur from Lower Normandy. The guests were silent, looking with a sort of terror at the pretty Comtesse d'Herouville. All were convinced that if such an event occurred, her savage lord would execute his threat.

The words of the count echoed in the bosom of the young wife, then pregnant; one of those presentiments which furrow a track like lightning through the soul, told her that her child would be born at seven months. An inward heat overflowed her from head to foot, sending the life's blood to her heart with such violence that the surface of her body felt bathed in ice. From that hour not a day had passed that the sense of secret terror did not check every impulse of her innocent gaiety. The memory of the look, of the inflections of voice with which the count accompanied his words, still froze her blood, and silenced her sufferings, as she leaned over that sleeping head, and strove to see some sign of a pity she had vainly sought there when awake.

The child, threatened with death before its life began, made so vigorous a movement that she cried aloud, in a voice that seemed like a sigh, "Poor babe!"

She said no more; there are ideas that a mother cannot bear. Incapable of reasoning at this moment, the countess was almost choked with the intensity of a suffering as yet unknown to her. Two tears, escaping from her eyes, rolled slowly down her cheeks, and traced two shining lines, remaining suspended at the bottom of that white face, like dewdrops on a lily. What learned man would take upon himself to say that

Honore de Balzac

the child unborn is on some neutral ground, where the emotions of its mother do not penetrate during those hours when soul clasps body and communicates its impressions, when thought permeates blood with healing balm or poisonous fluids? The terror that shakes the tree, will it not hurt the fruit? Those words, "Poor babe!" were they dictated by a vision of the future? The shuddering of this mother was violent; her look piercing.

The bloody answer given by the count at the banquet was a link mysteriously connecting the past with this premature confinement. That odious suspicion, thus publicly expressed, had cast into the memories of the countess a dread which echoed to the future. Since that fatal gala, she had driven from her mind, with as much fear as another woman would have found pleasure in evoking them, a thousand scattered scenes of her past existence. She refused even to think of the happy days when her heart was free to love. Like as the melodies of their native land make exiles weep, so these memories revived sensations so delightful that her young conscience thought them crimes, and sued them to enforce still further the savage threat of the count. There lay the secret of the horror which was now oppressing her soul.

Sleeping figures possess a sort of suavity, due to the absolute repose of both body and mind; but though that species of calmness softened but slightly the harsh expression of the count's features, all illusion granted to the unhappy is so persuasive that the poor wife ended by finding hope in that tranquillity. The roar of the tempest, now descending in torrents of rain, seemed to her no more than a melancholy moan; her fears and her pains both yielded her a momentary respite. Contemplating the man to whom her life was bound, the countess allowed herself to float into a reverie, the sweetness of which was so intoxicating that she had no strength to break its charm. For a moment, by one of those visions which in some way share the divine power, there passed before her rapid images of a happiness lost beyond recall.

Jeanne in her vision saw faintly, and as if in a distant gleam of dawn, the modest castle where her careless childhood had glided on; there were the verdant lawns, the rippling brook, the little chamber, the scenes of her happy play. She saw herself gathering flowers and planting them, unknowing why they wilted and would not grow, despite her constancy in watering them. Next, she saw confusedly the vast town and the vast house blackened by age, to which her mother took her when she was seven years old. Her lively memory showed her the old gray heads of the masters who taught and tormented her. She remembered the person of her father; she saw him getting off his mule at the door of the manor-house, and taking her by the hand to lead her up the stairs; she recalled how her prattle drove from his brow the judicial cares he did not always lay aside with his black or his red robes, the white fur of which fell one day by chance under the snipping of her mischievous scissors. She cast but one glance at the confessor of her aunt, the mother-superior of a convent of Poor Clares, a rigid and fanatical old man, whose duty it was to initiate her into the mysteries of religion. Hardened by the severities necessary against heretics, the old priest never ceased to jangle the chains of hell; he told her of nothing but the vengeance of Heaven, and made her tremble with the assurance that God's eye was on her. Rendered timid, she dared not raise her eyes in the priest's presence, and ceased to have any feeling but respect for her mother, whom up to that time she had made a sharer in all her frolics. When she saw that beloved mother turning her blue eyes towards her with an appearance of anger, a religious terror took possession of the girl's heart.

Then suddenly the vision took her to the second period of her childhood, when as yet she understood nothing of the things of life. She thought with an almost mocking regret of the days when all her happiness was to work beside her mother in the tapestried salon, to pray in the church, to sing her ballads to a lute, to read in secret a romance of chivalry, to pluck the petals of a flower, discover what gift her father would make her on the feast of the Blessed Saint-John, and find out the meaning of speeches repressed before her. Passing thus from her childish joys through the sixteen years of her girlhood, the grace of those softly flowing years when she knew no pain was eclipsed by the brightness of a memory precious though ill-fated. The joyous peace of her childhood was far less sweet to her than a single one of the troubles scattered upon the last two years of her childhood, - years that were rich in treasures now buried forever in her heart.

The vision brought her suddenly to that morning, that ravishing morning, when in the grand old parlor panelled and carved in oak, which served the family as a dining-room, she saw her handsome cousin for the first time. Alarmed by the seditions in Paris, her mother's family had sent the young courtier to Rouen, hoping that he could there be trained to the duties of the magistracy by his uncle, whose office might some day devolve upon him. The countess smiled involuntarily as she remembered the haste with which she retired on seeing this relation whom she did not know. But, in spite of the rapidity with which she opened and shut the door, a single glance had put into her soul so vigorous an impression of the scene that even at this moment she seemed to see it still occurring. Her eye again wandered from the violet velvet mantle embroidered with gold and lined with satin to the spurs on the boots, the pretty lozenges slashed into the doublet, the trunk-hose, and the rich collaret which gave to view a throat as white as the lace around it. She stroked with her hand the handsome face with its tiny pointed moustache, and "royale" as small as the ermine tips upon her father's hood.

In the silence of the night, with her eyes fixed on the green silk curtains which she no longer saw, the countess, forgetting the storm, her husband, and her fears, recalled the days which seemed to her longer than years, so full were they, - days when she loved, and was beloved! - and the moment when, fearing her mother's sternness, she had slipped one morning into her father's study to whisper her girlish confidences on his knee, waiting for his smile at her caresses to say in his ear, "Will you scold me if I tell you something?" Once more she heard her father say, after a few questions in reply to which she spoke for the first time of her love, "Well, well, my child, we will think of it. If he studies well, if he fits himself to succeed me, if he continues to please you, I will be on your side."

After that she had listened no longer; she had kissed her father, and, knocking over his papers as she ran from the room, she flew to the great linden-tree where, daily, before her formidable mother rose, she met that charming cousin, Georges de Chaverny.

Faithfully the youth promised to study law and customs. He laid aside the splendid trappings of the nobility of the sword to wear the sterner costume of the magistracy.

"I like you better in black," she said.

It was a falsehood, but by that falsehood she comforted her lover for having thrown his dagger to the winds. The memory of the little schemes employed to deceive her mother, whose severity seemed great, brought back to her the soulful joys of that innocent and mutual and sanctioned love; sometimes a rendezvous beneath the linden, where speech could be freer than before witnesses; sometimes a furtive clasp, or a stolen kiss, - in short, all the naive instalments of a passion that did not pass the bounds of modesty. Reliving in her vision those delightful days when she seemed to have too much happiness, she fancied that she kissed, in the void, that fine young face with the glowing eyes, that rosy mouth that spoke so well of love. Yes, she had loved Chaverny, poor apparently; but what treasures had she not discovered in that soul as tender as it was strong!

Suddenly her father died. Chaverny did not succeed him. The flames of civil war burst forth. By Chaverny's care she and her mother found refuge in a little town of Lower Normandy. Soon the deaths of other relatives made her one of the richest heiresses in France. Happiness disappeared as wealth came to her. The savage and terrible face of Comte d'Herouville, who asked her hand, rose before her like a thunder-cloud, spreading its gloom over the smiling meadows so lately gilded by the sun. The poor countess strove to cast from her memory the scenes of weeping and despair brought about by her long resistance.

At last came an awful night when her mother, pale and dying, threw herself at her daughter's feet. Jeanne could save Chaverny's life by yielding; she yielded. It was night. The count, arriving bloody from the battle-field was there; all was ready, the priest, the altar, the torches! Jeanne belonged henceforth to misery. Scarcely had she time to say to her young cousin who was set at liberty: -

"Georges, if you love me, never see me again!"

She heard the departing steps of her lover, whom, in truth, she never saw again; but in the depths of her heart she still kept sacred his last look which returned perpetually in her dreams and illumined them. Living like a cat shut into a lion's cage, the young wife dreaded at all hours the claws of the master which ever threatened her. She knew that in order to be happy she must forget the past and think only of the future; but there were days, consecrated to the memory of some vanished joy, when she deliberately made it a crime to put on the gown she had worn on the day she had seen her lover for the first time.

"I am not guilty," she said, "but if I seem guilty to the count it is as if I were so. Perhaps I am! The Holy Virgin conceived without -"

She stopped. During this moment when her thoughts were misty and her soul floated in a region of fantasy her naivete made her attribute to that last look with which her lover transfixed her the occult power of the visitation of the angel to the Mother of her Lord. This supposition, worthy of the days of innocence to which

Honore de Balzac

her reverie had carried her back, vanished before the memory of a conjugal scene more odious than death. The poor countess could have no real doubt as to the legitimacy of the child that stirred in her womb. The night of her marriage reappeared to her in all the horror if its agony, bringing in its train other such nights and sadder days.

"Ah! my poor Chaverny!" she cried, weeping, "you so respectful, so gracious, YOU were always kind to me."

She turned her eyes to her husband as if to persuade herself that that harsh face contained a promise of mercy, dearly brought. The count was awake. His yellow eyes, clear as those of a tiger, glittered beneath their tufted eyebrows and never had his glance been so incisive. The countess, terrified at having encountered it, slid back under the great counterpane and was motionless.

"Why are you weeping?" said the count, pulling away the covering which hid his wife.

That voice, always a terror to her, had a specious softness at this moment which seemed to her of good augury.

"I suffer much," she answered.

"Well, my pretty one, it is no crime to suffer; why did you tremble when I looked at you? Alas! what must I do to be loved?" The wrinkles of his forehead between the eyebrows deepened. "I see plainly you are afraid of me," he added, sighing.

Prompted by the instinct of feeble natures the countess

interrupted the count by moans, exclaiming: -

"I fear a miscarriage! I clambered over the rocks last evening and tired myself."

Hearing those words, the count cast so horribly suspicious a look upon his wife, that she reddened and shuddered. He mistook the fear of the innocent creature for remorse.

"Perhaps it is the beginning of a regular childbirth," he said.

"What then?" she said.

"In any case, I must have a proper man here," he said. "I will fetch one."

The gloomy look which accompanied these words overcame the countess, who fell back in the bed with a moan, caused more by a sense of her fate than by the agony of the coming crisis; that moan convinced the count of the justice of the suspicions that were rising in his mind. Affecting a calmness which the tones of his voice, his gestures, and looks contradicted, he rose hastily, wrapped himself in a dressing-gown which lay on a chair, and began by locking a door near the chimney through which the state bedroom was entered from the reception rooms which communicated with the great staircase.

Seeing her husband pocket that key, the countess had a presentiment of danger. She next heard him open the door opposite to that which he had just locked and enter a room where the counts of Herouville slept when they did not honor their wives with their noble

Honore de Balzac

company. The countess knew of that room only by
hearsay. Jealousy kept her husband always with her. If
occasionally some military expedition forced him to
leave her, the count left more than one Argus, whose
incessant spying proved his shameful distrust.

In spite of the attention the countess now gave to the
slightest noise, she heard nothing more. The count had,
in fact, entered a long gallery leading from his room
which continued down the western wing of the castle.
Cardinal d'Herouville, his great-uncle, a passionate
lover of the works of printing, had there collected a
library as interesting for the number as for the beauty
of its volumes, and prudence had caused him to build
into the walls one of those curious inventions suggested by solitude or by monastic fears. A silver chain
set in motion, by means of invisible wires, a bell
placed at the bed's head of a faithful servitor. The
count now pulled the chain, and the boots and spurs of
the man on duty sounded on the stone steps of a spiral
staircase, placed in the tall tower which flanked the
western corner of the chateau on the ocean side.

When the count heard the steps of his retainer he
pulled back the rusty bolts which protected the door
leading from the gallery to the tower, admitting into
the sanctuary of learning a man of arms whose stalwart
appearance was in keeping with that of his master.
This man, scarcely awakened, seemed to have walked
there by instinct; the horn lantern which he held in his
hand threw so feeble a gleam down the long library
that his master and he appeared in that visible darkness
like two phantoms.

"Saddle my war-horse instantly, and come with me
yourself."

This order was given in a deep tone which roused the man's intelligence. He raised his eyes to those of his master and encountered so piercing a look that the effect was that of an electric shock.

"Bertrand," added the count laying his right hand on the servant's arm, "take off your cuirass, and wear the uniform of a captain of guerrillas."

"Heavens and earth, monseigneur! What? disguise myself as a Leaguer! Excuse me, I will obey you; but I would rather be hanged."

The count smiled; then to efface that smile, which contrasted with the expression of his face, he answered roughly: -

"Choose the strongest horse there is in the stable and follow me. We shall ride like balls shot from an arque- buse. Be ready when I am ready. I will ring to let you know."

Bertrand bowed in silence and went away; but when he had gone a few steps he said to himself, as he listened to the howling of the storm: -

"All the devils are abroad, jarnidieu! I'd have been surprised to see this one stay quietly in his bed. We took Saint-Lo in just such a tempest as this."

The count kept in his room a disguise which often served him in his campaign stratagems. Putting on the shabby buff-coat that looked as thought it might belong to one of the poor horse-soldiers whose pittance was so seldom paid by Henri IV., he returned to the room where his wife was moaning.

"Try to suffer patiently," he said to her. "I will founder my horse if necessary to bring you speedy relief."

These words were certainly not alarming, and the countess, emboldened by them, was about to make a request when the count asked her suddenly: -

"Tell me where you keep your masks?"

"My masks!" she replied. "Good God! what do you want to do with them?"

"Where are they?" he repeated, with his usual violence.

"In the chest," she said.

She shuddered when she saw her husband select from among her masks a "touret de nez," the wearing of which was as common among the ladies of that time as the wearing of gloves in our day. The count became entirely unrecognizable after he had put on an old gray felt hat with a broken cock's feather on his head. He girded round his loins a broad leathern belt, in which he stuck a dagger, which he did not wear habitually. These miserable garments gave him so terrifying an air and he approached the bed with so strange a motion that the countess thought her last hour had come.

"Ah! don't kill us!" she cried, "leave me my child, and I will love you well."

"You must feel yourself very guilty to offer as the ransom of your faults the love you owe me."

The count's voice was lugubrious and the bitter words were enforced by a look which fell like lead upon the countess.

"My God!" she cried sorrowfully, "can innocence be fatal?"

"Your death is not in question," said her master, coming out of a sort of reverie into which he had fallen. "You are to do exactly, and for love of me, what I shall now tell you."

He flung upon the bed one of the two masks he had taken from the chest, and smiled with derision as he saw the gesture of involuntary fear which the slight shock of the black velvet wrung from his wife.

"You will give me a puny child!" he cried. "Wear that mask on your face when I return. I'll have no barber-surgeon boast that he has seen the Comtesse d'Herouville."

"A man! - why choose a man for the purpose?" she said in a feeble voice.

"Ho! ho! my lady, am I not master here?" replied the count.

"What matters one horror the more!" murmured the countess; but her master had disappeared, and the exclamation did her no injury.

Presently, in a brief lull of the storm, the countess heard the gallop of two horses which seemed to fly across the sandy dunes by which the castle was surrounded. The sound was quickly lost in that of the waves. Soon she felt herself a prisoner in the vast apartment, alone in the midst of a night both silent and threatening, and without succor against an evil she saw approaching her with rapid strides. In vain she sought for some stratagem by which to save that child conceived in tears, already her consolation, the spring of all her thoughts, the future of her affections, her one frail hope.

Sustained by maternal courage, she took the horn with which her husband summoned his men, and, opening a window, blew through the brass tube feeble notes that died away upon the vast expanse of water, like a bubble blown into the air by a child. She felt the uselessness of that moan unheard of men, and turned to hasten through the apartments, hoping that all the issues were not closed upon her. Reaching the library she sought in vain for some secret passage; then, passing between the long rows of books, she reached a window which looked upon the courtyard. Again she sounded the horn, but without success against the voice of the hurricane.

In her helplessness she thought of trusting herself to one of the women, - all creatures of her husband, - when, passing into her oratory, she found that the count had locked the only door that led to their apartments. This was a horrible discovery. Such precautions taken to isolate her showed a desire to proceed without witnesses to some horrible execution. As moment after moment she lost hope, the pangs of childbirth grew stronger and keener. A presentiment of murder, joined to the fatigue of her efforts, overcame her last remaining strength. She was like a ship-wrecked man who sinks, borne under by one last wave less furious than others he has vanquished. The bewildering pangs of her condition kept her from knowing the lapse of time. At the moment when she felt that, alone, without help, she was about to give birth to her child, and to all her other terrors was added that of the accidents to which her ignorance exposed her, the count appeared, without a sound that let her know of his arrival. The man was there, like a demon claiming at the close of a compact the soul that was sold to him. He muttered angrily at finding his wife's face uncovered; then after masking her carefully, he took her in his arms and laid her on the bed in her chamber.

CHAPTER II

THE BONESETTER

The terror of that apparition and hasty removal stopped for a moment the physical sufferings of the countess, and so enabled her to cast a furtive glance at the actors in this mysterious scene. She did not recognize Bertrand, who was there disguised and masked as carefully as his master. After lighting in haste some candles, the light of which mingled with the first rays of the sun which were reddening the window panes, the old servitor had gone to the embrasure of a window and stood leaning against a corner of it. There, with his face towards the wall, he seemed to be estimating its thickness, keeping his body in such absolute immobility that he might have been taken for a statue. In the middle of the room the countess beheld a short, stout man, apparently out of breath and stupefied, whose eyes were blindfolded and his features so distorted with terror that it was impossible to guess at their natural expression.

"God's death! you scamp," said the count, giving him back his eyesight by a rough movement which threw upon the man's neck the bandage that had been upon his eyes. "I warn you not to look at anything but the wretched woman on whom you are now to exercise your skill; if you do, I'll fling you into the river that flows beneath those windows, with a collar round your neck weighing a hundred pounds!"

With that, he pulled down upon the breast of his stupefied hearer the cravat with which his eyes had been bandaged.

"Examine first if this can be a miscarriage," he continued; "in which case your life will answer to me for the mother's; but, if the child is living, you are to bring it to me."

So saying, the count seized the poor operator by the body and placed him before the countess, then he went himself to the depths of a bay-window and began to drum with his fingers upon the panes, casting glances alternately on his serving-man, on the bed, and at the ocean, as if he were pledging to the expected child a cradle in the waves.

The man whom, with outrageous violence, the count and Bertrand had snatched from his bed and fastened to the crupper of the latter's horse, was a personage whose individuality may serve to characterize the period, - a man, moreover, whose influence was destined to make itself felt in the house of Herouville.

Never in any age were the nobles so little informed as to natural science, and never was judicial astrology held in greater honor; for at no period in history was there a greater general desire to know the future. This ignorance and this curiosity had led to the utmost confusion in human knowledge; all things were still mere personal experience; the nomenclatures of theory did not exist; printing was done at enormous cost; scientific communication had little or no facility; the

Church persecuted science and all research which was based on the analysis of natural phenomena. Persecution begat mystery. So, to the people as well as to the nobles, physician and alchemist, mathematician and astronomer, astrologer and necromancer were six attributes, all meeting in the single person of the physician. In those days a superior physician was supposed to be cultivating magic; while curing his patient he was drawing their horoscopes. Princes protected the men of genius who were willing to reveal the future; they lodged them in their palaces and pensioned them. The famous Cornelius Agrippa, who came to France to become the physician of Henri II., would not consent, as Nostradamus did, to predict the future, and for this reason he was dismissed by Catherine de' Medici, who replaced him with Cosmo Ruggiero. The men of science, who were superior to their times, were therefore seldom appreciated; they simply inspired an ignorant fear of occult sciences and their results.

Without being precisely one of the famous mathematicians, the man whom the count had brought enjoyed in Normandy the equivocal reputation which attached to a physician who was known to do mysterious works. He belonged to the class of sorcerers who are still called in parts of France "bonesetters." This name belonged to certain untutored geniuses who, without apparent study, but by means of hereditary knowledge and the effect of long practice, the observations of which accumulated in the family, were bonesetters; that is, they mended broken limbs and cured both men and beasts of certain maladies, possessing secrets said to be marvellous for the treatment of serious cases. But not only had Maitre Antoine Beauvouloir (the name of the present bonesetter) a father and grandfather who were famous practitioners, from whom he inherited important traditions, he was also learned in medicine, and was given to the study of natural science. The country people saw his study full of books and other strange things which gave to his successes a coloring of magic. Without passing strictly for a sorcerer, Antoine Beauvouloir impressed the populace through a circumference of a hundred miles with respect akin to terror, and (what was far more really dangerous for himself) he held in his power many secrets of life and death which concerned the noble families of that region. Like his father and grandfather before him, he was celebrated for his skill in confinements and miscarriages. In those days of unbridled disorder, crimes were so frequent and passions so violent that the higher nobility often found itself compelled to initiate Maitre Antoine Beauvouloir into secrets both shameful and terrible. His discretion, so essential to his safety, was absolute; consequently his clients paid him well, and his hereditary practice greatly increased. Always on the road, sometimes roused in the dead of night, as on this occasion by the count, sometimes obliged to spend several days with certain great ladies, he had never married; in fact, his reputation had hindered certain young women from accepting him. Incapable of finding consolation in the practice of his profession, which gave him such power over feminine weakness, the poor bonesetter felt himself born for the joys of family and yet was unable to obtain them.

The good man's excellent heart was concealed by a misleading appearance of joviality in keeping with his puffy cheeks and rotund figure, the vivacity of his fat little body, and the frankness of his speech. He was anxious to marry that he might have a daughter who should transfer his property to some poor noble; he did not like his station as bonesetter and wished to rescue his family name from the position in which the prejudices of the times had placed it. He himself took willingly enough to the feasts and jovialities which usually followed his principal operations. The habit of being on such occasions the most important personage in the company, had added to his natural gaiety a sufficient dose of serious vanity. His impertinences were usually well received in crucial moments when it often pleased him to perform his operations with a certain slow majesty. He was, in other respects, as inquisitive as a nightingale, as greedy as a hound, and as garrulous as all diplomatists who talk incessantly and betray no secrets. In spite of these defects developed in him by the endless adventures into which his profession led him, Antoine Beauvouloir was held to be the least bad man in Normandy. Though he belonged to the small number of minds who are superior to their epoch, the strong good sense of a Norman countryman warned him to conceal the ideas he acquired and the truths he from time to time discovered.

As soon as he found himself placed by the count in presence of a woman in childbirth, the bonesetter recovered his presence of mind. He felt the pulse of the masked lady; not that he gave it a single thought, but under cover of that medical action he could reflect, and he did reflect on his own situation. In none of the shameful and criminal intrigues in which superior force had compelled him to act as a blind instrument, had precautions been taken with such mystery as in this case. Though his death had often been threatened as a means of assuring the secrecy of enterprises in which he had taken part against his will, his life had never been so endangered as at that moment. He resolved, before all things, to find out who it was who now employed him, and to discover the actual extent of his danger, in order to save, if possible, his own little person.

"What is the trouble?" he said to the countess in a low voice, as he placed her in a manner to receive his help.

"Do not give him the child -"

"Speak loud!" cried the count in thundering tones which prevented Beauvouloir from hearing the last word uttered by the countess. "If not," added the count who was careful to disguise his voice, "say your 'In manus.'"

"Complain aloud," said the leech to the lady; "cry! scream! Jarnidieu! that man has a necklace that won't fit you any better than me. Courage, my little lady!"

"Touch her lightly!" cried the count.

"Monsieur is jealous," said the operator in a shrill voice, fortunately drowned by the countess's cries.

For Maitre Beauvouloir's safety Nature was merciful. It was more a miscarriage than a regular birth, and the child was so puny that it caused little suffering to the mother.

"Holy Virgin!" cried the bonesetter, "it isn't a miscarriage, after all!"

The count made the floor shake as he stamped with rage. The countess pinched Beauvouloir.

"Ah! I see!" he said to himself. "It ought to be a premature birth, ought it?" he whispered to the countess, who replied with an affirmative sign, as if that gesture were the only language in which to express her thoughts.

"It is not all clear to me yet," thought the bonesetter.

Like all men in constant practice, he recognized at once a woman in her first trouble as he called it. Though the modest inexperience of certain gestures showed him the virgin ignorance of the countess, the mischievous operator exclaimed: -

"Madame is delivered as if she knew all about it!"

The count then said, with a calmness more terrifying than his anger: -

"Give me the child."

"Don't give it him, for the love of God!" cried the mother, whose almost savage cry awoke in the heart of the little man a courageous pity which attached him, more than he knew himself, to the helpless infant rejected by his father.

"The child is not yet born; you are counting your chicken before it is hatched," he said, coldly, hiding the infant.

Surprised to hear no cries, he examined the child, thinking it dead. The count, seeing the deception, sprang upon him with one bound.

"God of heaven! will you give it to me?" he cried,

snatching the hapless victim which uttered feeble cries.

"Take care; the child is deformed and almost lifeless; it is a seven months' child," said Beauvouloir clinging to the count's arm. Then, with a strength given to him by the excitement of his pity, he clung to the father's fingers, whispering in a broken voice: "Spare yourself a crime, the child cannot live."

"Wretch!" replied the count, from whose hands the bonesetter had wrenched the child, "who told you that I wished to kill my son? Could I not caress it?"

"Wait till he is eighteen years old to caress him in that way," replied Beauvouloir, recovering the sense of his importance. "But," he added, thinking of his own safety, for he had recognized the Comte d'Herouville, who in his rage had forgotten to disguise his voice, "have him baptized at once and do not speak of his danger to the mother, or you will kill her."

The gesture of satisfaction which escaped the count when the child's death was prophesied, suggested this speech to the bonesetter as the best means of saving the child at the moment. Beauvouloir now hastened to carry the infant back to its mother who had fainted, and he pointed to her condition reprovingly, to warn the count of the results of his violence. The countess had heard all; for in many of the great crises of life the human organs acquire an otherwise unknown delicacy. But the cries of the child, laid beside her on the bed, restored her to life as if by magic; she fancied she heard the voices of angels, when, under cover of the whimperings of the babe, the bonesetter said in her ear:

"Take care of him, and he'll live a hundred years.

Beauvouloir knows what he is talking about."

A celestial sigh, a silent pressure of the hand were the reward of the leech, who had looked to see, before yielding the frail little creature to its mother's embrace, whether that of the father had done no harm to its puny organization. The half-crazed motion with which the mother hid her son beside her and the threatening glance she cast upon the count through the eye-holes of her mask, made Beauvouloir shudder.

"She will die if she loses that child too soon," he said to the count.

During the latter part of this scene the lord of Herouville seemed to hear and see nothing. Rigid, and as if absorbed in meditation, he stood by the window drumming on its panes. But he turned at the last words uttered by the bonesetter, with an almost frenzied motion, and came to him with uplifted dagger.

"Miserable clown!" he cried, giving him the opprobrious name by which the Royalists insulted the Leaguers. "Impudent scoundrel! your science which makes you the accomplice of men who steal inheritances is all that prevents me from depriving Normandy of her sorcerer."

So saying, and to Beauvouloir's great satisfaction, the count replaced the dagger in its sheath.

"Could you not," continued the count, "find yourself for once in your life in the honorable company of a noble and his wife, without suspecting them of the base crimes and trickery of your own kind? Kill my son! take him from his mother! Where did you get such crazy ideas? Am I a madman? Why do you attempt to frighten me about the life of that vigorous child? Fool! I defy your silly talk - but remember this, since you are here, your miserable life shall answer for that of the mother and the child."

The bonesetter was puzzled by this sudden change in the count's intentions. This show of tenderness for the infant alarmed him far more than the impatient cruelty and savage indifference hitherto manifested by the count, whose tone in pronouncing the last words seemed to Beauvouloir to point to some better scheme for reaching his infernal ends. The shrewd practitioner turned this idea over in his mind until a light struck him.

"I have it!" he said to himself. "This great and good noble does not want to make himself odious to his wife; he'll trust to the vials of the apothecary. I must warn the lady to see to the food and medicine of her babe."

As he turned toward the bed, the count who had opened a closet, stopped him with an imperious gesture, holding out a purse. Beauvouloir saw within its red silk meshes a quantity of gold, which the count now flung to him contemptuously.

"Though you make me out a villain I am not released from the obligation of paying you like a lord. I shall not ask you to be discreet. This man here," (pointing to Bertrand) "will explain to you that there are rivers and trees everywhere for miserable wretches who chatter of me."

So saying the count advanced slowly to the bonesetter,

Honore de Balzac

pushed a chair noisily toward him, as if to invite him to sit down, as he did himself by the bedside; then he said to his wife in a specious voice: -

"Well, my pretty one, so we have a son; this is a joyful thing for us. Do you suffer much?"

"No," murmured the countess.

The evident surprise of the mother, and the tardy demonstrations of pleasure on the part of the father, convinced Beauvouloir that there was some incident behind all this which escaped his penetration. He persisted in his suspicion, and rested his hand on that of the young wife, less to watch her condition than to convey to her some advice.

"The skin is good, I fear nothing for madame. The milk fever will come, of course; but you need not be alarmed; that is nothing."

At this point the wily bonesetter paused, and pressed the hand of the countess to make her attentive to his words.

"If you wish to avoid all anxiety about your son, madame," he continued, "never leave him; suckle him yourself, and beware of the drugs of apothecaries. The mother's breast is the remedy for all the ills of infancy. I have seen many births of seven months' children, but I never saw any so little painful as this. But that is not surprising; the child is so small. You could put him in a wooden shoe! I am certain he doesn't weight more than sixteen ounces. Milk, milk, milk. Keep him always on your breast and you will save him."

These last words were accompanied by a significant pressure of the fingers. Disregarding the yellow flames flashing from the eyeholes of the count's mask, Beauvouloir uttered these words with the serious imperturbability of a man who intends to earn his money.

"Ho! ho! bonesetter, you are leaving your old felt hat behind you," said Bertrand, as the two left the bedroom together.

The reasons of the sudden mercy which the count had shown to his son were to be found in a notary's office. At the moment when Beauvouloir arrested his murderous hand avarice and the Legal Custom of Normandy rose up before him. Those mighty powers stiffened his fingers and silenced the passion of his hatred. One cried out to him, "The property of your wife cannot belong to the house of Herouville except through a male child." The other pointed to a dying countess and her fortune claimed by the collateral heirs of the Saint-Savins. Both advised him to leave to nature the extinction of that hated child, and to wait the birth of a second son who might be healthy and vigorous before getting rid of his wife and first-born. He saw neither wife nor child; he saw the estates only, and hatred was softened by ambition. The mother, who knew his nature, was even more surprised than the bonesetter, and she still retained her instinctive fears, showing them at times openly, for the courage of mothers seemed suddenly to have doubled her strength.

Honore de Balzac

CHAPTER III

THE MOTHER'S LOVE

For several days the count remained assiduously beside his wife, showing her attentions to which self-interest imparted a sort of tenderness. The countess saw, however, that she alone was the object of these attentions. The hatred of the father for his son showed itself in every detail; he abstained from looking at him or touching him; he would rise abruptly and leave the room if the child cried; in short, he seemed to endure it living only through the hope of seeing it die. But even this self-restraint was galling to the count. The day on which he saw that the mother's intelligent eye perceived, without fully comprehending, the danger that threatened her son, he announced his departure on the morning after the mass for her churching was solemnized, under pretext of rallying his forces to the support of the king.

Such were the circumstances which preceded and accompanied the birth of Etienne d'Herouville. If the count had no other reason for wishing the death of this disowned son poor Etienne would still have been the object of his aversion. In his eyes the misfortune of a rickety, sickly constitution was a flagrant offence to his self-love as a father. If he execrated handsome men, he also detested weakly ones, in whom mental capacity took the place of physical strength. To please him a man should be ugly in face, tall, robust, and ignorant. Etienne, whose debility would bow him, as it were, to the sedentary occupations of knowledge, was certain to find in his father a natural enemy. His struggle with that colossus began therefore from his cradle, and his sole support against that cruel antagonist was the heart of his mother whose love increased, by a tender law of nature, as perils threatened him.

Buried in solitude after the abrupt departure of the count, Jeanne de Saint-Savin owed to her child the only semblance of happiness that consoled her life. She loved him as women love the child of an illicit love; obliged to suckle him, the duty never wearied her. She would not let her women care for the child. She dressed and undressed him, finding fresh pleasures in every little care that he required. Happiness glowed upon her face as she obeyed the needs of the little being. As Etienne had come into the world prematurely, no clothes were ready for him, and those that were needed she made herself, - with what perfection, you know, ye mothers, who have worked in silence for a treasured child. The days had never hours long enough for these manifold occupations and the minute precautions of the nursing mother; those days fled by, laden with her secret content.

The counsel of the bonesetter still continued in the countess's mind. She feared for her child, and would gladly not have slept in order to be sure that no one approached him during her sleep; and she kept his cradle beside her bed. In the absence of the count she ventured to send for the bonesetter, whose name she had caught and remembered. To her, Beauvouloir was a being to whom she owed an untold debt of gratitude;

and she desired of all things to question him on certain points relating to her son. If an attempt were made to poison him, how should she foil it? In what way ought she to manage his frail constitution? Was it well to nurse him long? If she died, would Beauvouloir undertake the care of the poor child's health?

To the questions of the countess, Beauvouloir, deeply touched, replied that he feared, as much as she did, an attempt to poison Etienne; but there was, he assured her, no danger as long as she nursed the child; and in future, when obliged to feed him, she must taste the food herself.

"If Madame la comtesse," he said, "feels anything strange upon her tongue, a prickly, bitter, strong salt taste, reject the food. Let the child's clothes be washed under her own eye and let her keep the key of the chest which contains them. Should anything happen to the child send instantly to me."

These instructions sank deep into Jeanne's heart. She begged Beauvouloir to regard her always as one who would do him any service in her power. On that the poor man told her that she held his happiness in her hands.

Then he related briefly how the Comte d'Herouville had in his youth loved a courtesan, known by the name of La Belle Romaine, who had formerly belonged to the Cardinal of Lorraine. Abandoned by the count before very long, she had died miserably, leaving a child named Gertrude, who had been rescued by the Sisters of the Convent of Poor Clares, the Mother Superior of which was Mademoiselle de Saint-Savin, the countess's aunt. Having been called to treat

Gertrude for an illness, he, Beauvouloir, had fallen in love with her, and if Madame la comtesse, he said, would undertake the affair, she should not only more than repay him for what she thought he had done for her, but she would make him grateful to her for life. The count might, sooner or later, be brought to take an interest in so beautiful a daughter, and might protect her indirectly by making him his physician.

The countess, compassionate to all true love, promised to do her best, and pursued the affair so warmly that at the birth of her second son she did obtain from her husband a "dot" for the young girl, who was married soon after to Beauvouloir. The "dot" and his savings enabled the bonesetter to buy a charming estate called Forcalier near the castle of Herouville, and to give his life the dignity of a student and man of learning.

Comforted by the kind physician, the countess felt that to her were given joys unknown to other mothers. Mother and child, two feeble beings, seemed united in one thought, they understood each other long before language could interpret between them. From the moment when Etienne first turned his eyes on things about him with the stupid eagerness of a little child, his glance had rested on the sombre hangings of the castle walls. When his young ear strove to listen and to distinguish sounds, he heard the monotonous ebb and flow of the sea upon the rocks, as regular as the swinging of a pendulum. Thus places, sounds, and things, all that strikes the senses and forms the character, inclined him to melancholy. His mother, too, was doomed to live and die in the clouds of melancholy; and to him, from his birth up, she was the only being that existed on the earth, and filled for him the desert. Like all frail children, Etienne's attitude was passive, and in that he resembled his mother. The delicacy of his organs was such that a sudden noise, or the presence of a boisterous person gave him a sort of fever. He was like those little insects for whom God seems to temper the violence of the wind and the heat of the sun; incapable, like them, of struggling against the slightest obstacle, he yielded, as they do, without resistance or complaint, to everything that seemed to him aggressive. This angelic patience inspired in the mother a sentiment which took away all fatigue from the incessant care required by so frail a being.

Soon his precocious perception of suffering revealed to him the power that he had upon his mother; often he tried to divert her with caresses and make her smile at his play; and never did his coaxing hands, his stammered words, his intelligent laugh fail to rouse her from her reverie. If he was tired, his care for her kept him from complaining.

"Poor, dear, little sensitive!" cried the countess as he fell asleep tired with some play which had driven the sad memories from her mind, "how can you live in this world? who will understand you? who will love you? who will see the treasures hidden in that frail body? No one! Like me, you are alone on earth."

She sighed and wept. The graceful pose of her child lying on her knees made her smile sadly. She looked at him long, tasting one of those pleasures which are a secret between mothers and God. Etienne's weakness was so great that until he was a year and a half old she had never dared to take him out of doors; but now the faint color which tinted the whiteness of his skin like the petals of a wild rose, showed that life and health were already there.

One morning the countess, giving herself up to the glad joy of all mothers when their first child walks for the first time, was playing with Etienne on the floor when suddenly she heard the heavy step of a man upon the boards. Hardly had she risen with a movement of involuntary surprise, when the count stood before her. She gave a cry, but endeavored instantly to undo that involuntary wrong by going up to him and offering her forehead for a kiss.

"Why not have sent me notice of your return?" she said.

"My reception would have been more cordial, but less frank," he answered bitterly.

Suddenly he saw the child. The evident health in which he found it wrung from him a gesture of surprise mingled with fury. But he repressed his anger, and began to smile.

"I bring good news," he said. "I have received the governorship of Champagne and the king's promise to be made duke and peer. Moreover, we have inherited a princely fortune from your cousin; that cursed Huguenot, Georges de Chaverny is killed."

The countess turned pale and dropped into a chair. She saw the secret of the devilish smile on her husband's face.

"Monsieur," she said in a voice of emotion, "you know well that I loved my cousin Chaverny. You will answer to God for the pain you inflict upon me."

At these words the eye of the count glittered; his lips

Honore de Balzac

trembled, but he could not utter a word, so furious was he; he flung his dagger on the table with such violence that the metal resounded like a thunder-clap.

"Listen to me," he said in his strongest voice, "and remember my words. I will never see or hear the little monster you hold in your arms. He is your child, and not mine; there is nothing of me in him. Hide him, I say, hide him from my sight, or -"

"Just God!" cried the countess, "protect us!"

"Silence!" said her husband. "If you do not wish me to throttle him, see that I never find him in my way."

"Then," said the countess gathering strength to oppose her tyrant, "swear to me that if you never meet him you will do nothing to injure him. Can I trust your word as a nobleman for that?"

"What does all this mean?" said the count.

"If you will not swear, kill us now together!" cried the countess, falling on her knees and pressing her child to her breast.

"Rise, madame. I give you my word as a man of honor to do nothing against the life of that cursed child, provided he lives among the rocks between the sea and the house, and never crosses my path. I will give him that fisherman's house down there for his dwelling, and the beach for a domain. But woe betide him if I ever find him beyond those limits."

The countess began to weep.

"Look at him!" she said. "He is your son."

"Madame!"

At that word, the frightened mother carried away the child whose heart was beating like that of a bird caught in its nest. Whether innocence has a power which the hardest men cannot escape, or whether the count regretted his violence and feared to plunge into despair a creature so necessary to his pleasures and also to his worldly prosperity, it is certain that his voice was as soft as it was possible to make it when his wife returned.

"Jeanne, my dear," he said, "do not be angry with me; give me your hand. One never knows how to trust you women. I return, bringing you fresh honors and more wealth, and yet, tete-Dieu! you receive me like an enemy. My new government will oblige me to make long absences until I can exchange it for that of Lower Normandy; and I request, my dear, that you will show me a pleasant face while I am here."

The countess understood the meaning of the words, the feigned softness of which could no longer deceive her.

"I know my duty," she replied in a tone of sadness which the count mistook for tenderness.

The timid creature had too much purity and dignity to try, as some clever women would have done, to govern the count by putting calculation into her conduct, - a sort of prostitution by which noble souls feel degraded. Silently she turned away, to console her despair with Etienne.

"Tete-Dieu! shall I never be loved?" cried the count, seeing the tears in his wife's eyes as she left the room.

Thus incessantly threatened, motherhood became to the poor woman a passion which assumed the intensity that women put into their guilty affections. By a species of occult communion, the secret of which is in the hearts of mothers, the child comprehended the peril that threatened him and dreaded the approach of his father. The terrible scene of which he had been a witness remained in his memory, and affected him like an illness; at the sound of the count's step his features contracted, and the mother's ear was not so alert as the instinct of her child. As he grew older this faculty created by terror increased, until, like the savages of America, Etienne could distinguish his father's step and hear his voice at immense distances. To witness the terror with which the count inspired her thus shared by her child made Etienne the more precious to the countess; their union was so strengthened that like two flowers on one twig they bent to the same wind, and lifted their heads with the same hope. In short, they were one life.

When the count again left home Jeanne was pregnant. This time she gave birth in due season, and not without great suffering, to a stout boy, who soon became the living image of his father, so that the hatred of the count for his first-born was increased by this event. To save her cherished child the countess agreed to all the plans which her husband formed for the happiness and wealth of his second son, whom he named Maximilien. Etienne was to be made a priest, in order to leave the property and titles of the house of Herouville to his younger brother. At that cost the poor mother believed she ensured the safety of her hated child.

No two brothers were ever more unlike than Etienne
and Maximilien. The younger's taste was all for noise,
violent exercises, and war, and the count felt for him
the same excessive love that his wife felt for Etienne.
By a tacit compact each parent took charge of the child
of their heart. The duke (for about this time Henri IV.
rewarded the services of the Seigneur d'Herouville
with a dukedom), not wishing, he said, to fatigue his
wife, gave the nursing of the youngest boy to a stout
peasant-woman chosen by Beauvouloir, and announced his determination to bring up the child in his
own manner. He gave him, as time went on, a holy
horror of books and study; taught him the mechanical
knowledge required by a military career, made him a
good rider, a good shot with an arquebuse, and skilful
with his dagger. When the boy was big enough he took
him to hunt, and let him acquire the savage language,
the rough manners, the bodily strength, and the
vivacity of look and speech which to his mind were the
attributes of an accomplished man. The boy became,
by the time he was twelve years old, a lion-cub ill-
trained, as formidable in his way as the father himself,
having free rein to tyrannize over every one, and using
the privilege.

Etienne lived in the little house, or lodge, near the sea,
given to him by his father, and fitted up by the duchess
with some of the comforts and enjoyments to which he
had a right. She herself spent the greater part of her
time there. Together the mother and child roamed over
the rocks and the shore, keeping strictly within the
limits of the boy's domain of beach and shells, of moss
and pebbles. The boy's terror of his father was so great
that, like the Lapp, who lives and dies in his snow, he
made a native land of his rocks and his cottage, and
was terrified and uneasy if he passed his frontier.

The duchess, knowing her child was not fitted to find happiness except in some humble and retired sphere, did not regret the fate that was thus imposed upon him; she used this enforced vocation to prepare him for a noble life of study and science, and she brought to the chateau Pierre de Sebonde as tutor to the future priest. Nevertheless, in spite of the tonsure imposed by the will of the father, she was determined that Etienne's education should not be wholly ecclesiastical, and took pains to secularize it. She employed Beauvouloir to teach him the mysteries of natural science; she herself superintended his studies, regulating them according to her child's strength, and enlivening them by teaching him Italian, and revealing to him little by little the poetic beauties of that language. While the duke rode off with Maximilien to the forest and the wild-boars at the risk of his life, Jeanne wandered with Etienne in the milky way of Petrarch's sonnets, or the mighty labyrinth of the Divina Comedia. Nature had endowed the youth, in compensation for his infirmities, with so melodious a voice that to hear him sing was a constant delight; his mother taught him music, and their tender, melancholy songs, accompanied by a mandolin, were the favorite recreation promised as a reward for some more arduous study required by the Abbe de Sebonde. Etienne listened to his mother with a passionate admiration she had never seen except in the eyes of Georges de Chaverny. The first time the poor woman found a memory of her girlhood in the long, slow look of her child, she covered him with kisses; and she blushed when Etienne asked her why she seemed to love him better at that moment than ever before. She answered that every hour made him dearer to her. She found in the training of his soul, and in the culture of his mind, pleasures akin to those she had tasted in feeding him with her milk. She put all her pride and self-love into making him superior to herself, and not in ruling him. Hearts without tenderness covet dominion, but a true love treasures abnegation, that virtue of strength. When Etienne could not at first comprehend a demonstration, a theme, a theory, the poor mother, who was present at the lessons, seemed to long to infuse knowledge, as formerly she had given nourishment at the child's least cry. And then, what joy suffused her eyes when Etienne's mind seized the true sense of things and appropriated it. She proved, as Pierre de Sebonde said, that a mother is a dual being whose sensations cover two existences.

"Ah, if some woman as loving as I could infuse into him hereafter the life of love, how happy he might be!" she often thought.

But the fatal interests which consigned Etienne to the priesthood returned to her mind, and she kissed the hair that the scissors of the Church were to shear, leaving her tears upon them. Still, in spite of the unjust compact she had made with the duke, she could not see Etienne in her visions of the future as priest or cardinal; and the absolute forgetfulness of the father as to his first-born, enabled her to postpone the moment of putting him into Holy Orders.

"There is time enough," she said to herself.

The day came when all her cares, inspired by a sentiment which seemed to enter into the flesh of her son and give it life, had their reward. Beauvouloir - that blessed man whose teachings had proved so precious to the child, and whose anxious glance at that frail idol had so often made the duchess tremble - declared that Etienne was now in a condition to live long years, provided no violent emotion came to convulse his delicate body. Etienne was then sixteen.

At that age he was just five feet, a height he never passed. His skin, as transparent and satiny as that of a little girl, showed a delicate tracery of blue veins; its whiteness was that of porcelain. His eyes, which were light blue and ineffably gentle, implored the protection of men and women; that beseeching look fascinated before the melody of his voice was heard to complete the charm. True modesty was in every feature. Long chestnut hair, smooth and very fine, was parted in the middle of his head into two bandeaus which curled at their extremity. His pale and hollow cheeks, his pure brow, lined with a few furrows, expressed a condition of suffering which was painful to witness. His mouth, always gracious, and adorned with very white teeth, wore the sort of fixed smile which we often see on the lips of the dying. His hands, white as those of a woman, were remarkably handsome. The habit of meditation had taught him to droop his head like a fragile flower, and the attitude was in keeping with his person; it was like the last grace that a great artist touches into a portrait to bring out its latent thought. Etienne's head was that of a delicate girl placed upon the weakly and deformed body of a man.

Poesy, the rich meditations of which make us roam like botanists through the vast fields of thought, the fruitful comparison of human ideas, the enthusiasm given by a clear conception of works of genius, came to be the inexhaustible and tranquil joys of the young man's solitary and dreamy life. Flowers, ravishing creatures whose destiny resembled his own, were his loves. Happy to see in her son the innocent passions which took the place of the rough contact with social life which he never could have borne, the duchess encouraged Etienne's tastes; she brought him Spanish "romanceros," Italian "motets," books, sonnets, poems. The library of Cardinal d'Herouville came into Etienne's possession, the use of which filled his life. These readings, which his fragile health forbade him to continue for many hours at a time, and his rambles among the rocks of his domain, were interspersed with naive meditations which kept him motionless for hours together before his smiling flowers - those sweet companions! - or crouching in a niche of the rocks before some species of algae, a moss, a seaweed, studying their mysteries; seeking perhaps a rhythm in their fragrant depths, like a bee its honey. He often admired, without purpose, and without explaining his pleasure to himself, the slender lines on the petals of dark flowers, the delicacy of their rich tunics of gold or purple, green or azure, the fringes, so profusely beautiful, of their calyxes or leaves, their ivory or velvet textures. Later, a thinker as well as a poet, he would detect the reason of these innumerable differences in a single nature, by discovering the indication of unknown faculties; for from day to day he made progress in the interpretation of the Divine Word writing upon all things here below.

These constant and secret researches into matters occult gave to Etienne's life the apparent somnolence of meditative genius. He would spend long days lying upon the shore, happy, a poet, all-unconscious of the fact. The sudden irruption of a gilded insect, the shimmering of the sun upon the ocean, the tremulous motion of the vast and limpid mirror of the waters, a shell, a crab, all was event and pleasure to that ingenuous young soul. And then to see his mother coming towards him, to hear from afar the rustle of her gown, to await her, to kiss her, to talk to her, to listen to her gave him such keen emotions that often a slight delay, a trifling fear would throw him into a violent fever. In him there was nought but soul, and in order that the weak, debilitated body should not be destroyed by the keen emotions of that soul, Etienne needed silence, caresses, peace in the landscape, and the love of a woman. For the time being, his mother gave him the love and the caresses; flowers and books entranced his solitude; his little kingdom of sand and shells, algae and verdure seemed to him a universe, ever fresh and new.

Etienne imbibed all the benefits of this physical and absolutely innocent life, this mental and moral life so poetically extended. A child by form, a man in mind, he was equally angelic under either aspect. By his mother's influence his studies had removed his emotions to the region of ideas. The action of his life took place, therefore, in the moral world, far from the social world which would either have killed him or made him suffer. He lived by his soul and by his intellect. Laying hold of human thought by reading, he rose to thoughts that stirred in matter; he felt the thoughts of the air, he read the thoughts on the skies. Early he mounted that ethereal summit where alone he found the delicate nourishment that his soul needed; intoxicating food! which predestined him to sorrow whenever to these accumulated treasures should be added the riches of a passion rising suddenly in his heart.

If, at times, Jeanne de Saint-Savin dreaded that coming storm, he consoled herself with a thought which the otherwise sad vocation of her son put into her mind, - for the poor mother found no remedy for his sorrows except some lesser sorrow.

"He will be a cardinal," she thought; "he will live in the sentiment of Art, of which he will make himself the protector. He will love Art instead of loving a woman, and Art will not betray him."

The pleasures of this tender motherhood were incessantly held in check by sad reflections, born of the strange position in which Etienne was placed. The brothers had passed the adolescent age without knowing each other, without so much as even suspecting their rival existence. The duchess had long hoped for an opportunity, during the absence of her husband, to bind the two brothers to each other in some solemn scene by which she might enfold them both in her love. This hope, long cherished, had now faded. Far from wishing to bring about an intercourse between the brothers, she feared an encounter between them, even more than between the father and son. Maximilien, who believed in evil only, might have feared that Etienne would some day claim his rights, and, so fearing, might have flung him into the sea with a stone around his neck. No son had ever less respect for a mother than he. As soon as he could reason he had seen the low esteem in which the duke held his wife. If the old man still retained some forms of decency in his manners to the duchess, Maximilien, unrestrained by his father, caused his mother many a grief.

Consequently, Bertrand was incessantly on the watch to prevent Maximilien from seeing Etienne, whose existence was carefully concealed. All the attendants of the castle cordially hated the Marquis de Saint-Sever (the name and title borne by the younger brother), and those who knew of the existence of the elder looked upon him as an avenger whom God was holding in reserve.

Etienne's future was therefore doubtful; he might even be persecuted by his own brother! The poor duchess had no relations to whom she could confide the life and interests of her cherished child. Would he not blame her when in his violet robes he longed to be a father as she had been a mother? These thoughts, and her melancholy life so full of secret sorrows were like a mortal illness kept at bay for a time by remedies. Her heart needed the wisest management, and those about her were cruelly inexpert in gentleness. What mother's heart would not have been torn at the sight of her eldest son, a man of mind and soul in whom a noble genius made itself felt, deprived of his rights, while the younger, hard and brutal, without talent, even military talent, was chosen to wear the ducal coronet and perpetuate the family? The house of Herouville was discarding its own glory. Incapable of anger the gentle Jeanne de Saint-Savin could only bless and weep, but often she raised her eyes to heaven, asking it to account for this singular doom. Those eyes filled with tears when she thought that at her death her cherished child would be wholly orphaned and left exposed to the brutalities of a brother without faith or conscience.

Such emotions repressed, a first love unforgotten, so many sorrows ignored and hidden within her, - for she kept her keenest sufferings from her cherished child, - her joys embittered, her griefs unrelieved, all these shocks had weakened the springs of life and were developing in her system a slow consumption which day by day was gathering greater force. A last blow hastened it. She tried to warn the duke as to the results of Maximilien's education, and was repulsed; she saw that she could give no remedy to the shocking seeds which were germinating in the soul of her second child. From this moment began a period of decline which soon became so visible as to bring about the appointment of Beauvouloir to the post of physician to the house of Herouville and the government of Normandy.

The former bonesetter came to live at the castle. In those days such posts belonged to learned men, who thus gained a living and the leisure necessary for a studious life and the accomplishment of scientific work. Beauvouloir had for some time desired the situation, because his knowledge and his fortune had won him numerous bitter enemies. In spite of the protection of a great family to whom he had done great services, he had recently been implicated in a criminal case, and the intervention of the Governor of Normandy, obtained by the duchess, had alone saved him from being brought to trial. The duke had no reason to repent this protection given to the old bone-setter. Beauvouloir saved the life of the Marquis de Saint-Sever in so dangerous an illness that any other physician would have failed in doing so. But the wounds of the duchess were too deep-seated and dated too far back to be cured, especially as they were constantly kept open in her home. When her sufferings warned this angel of many sorrows that her end was approaching, death was hastened by the gloomy apprehensions that filled her mind as to the future.

"What will become of my poor child without me?" was a thought renewed every hour like a bitter tide.

Obliged at last to keep her bed, the duchess failed rapidly, for she was then unable to see her son,

Honore de Balzac

forbidden as he was by her compact with his father to approach the house. The sorrow of the youth was equal to that of the mother. Inspired by the genius of repressed feeling, Etienne created a mystical language by which to communicate with his mother. He studied the resources of his voice like an opera-singer, and often he came beneath her windows to let her hear his melodiously melancholy voice, when Beauvouloir by a sign informed him she was alone. Formerly, as a babe, he had consoled his mother with his smiles, now, become a poet, he caressed her with his melodies.

"Those songs give me life," said the duchess to Beauvouloir, inhaling the air that Etienne's voice made living.

At length the day came when the poor son's mourning began. Already he had felt the mysterious correspondences between his emotions and the movements of the ocean. The divining of the thoughts of matter, a power with which his occult knowledge had invested him, made this phenomenon more eloquent to him than to all others. During the fatal night when he was taken to see his mother for the last time, the ocean was agitated by movements that to him were full of meaning. The heaving waters seemed to show that the sea was working intestinally; the swelling waves rolled in and spent themselves with lugubrious noises like the howling of a dog in distress. Unconsciously, Etienne found himself saying: -

"What does it want of me? It quivers and moans like a living creature. My mother has often told me that the ocean was in horrible convulsions on the night when I was born. Something is about to happen to me."

This thought kept him standing before his window with his eyes sometimes on his mother's windows where a faint light trembled, sometimes on the ocean which continued to moan. Suddenly Beauvouloir knocked on the door of his room, opened it, and showed on his saddened face the reflection of some new misfortune.

"Monseigneur," he said, "Madame la duchesse is in so sad a state that she wishes to see you. All precautions are taken that no harm shall happen to you in the castle; but we must be prudent; to see her you will have to pass through the room of Monseigneur the duke, the room where you were born."

These words brought the tears to Etienne's eyes, and he said: -

"The Ocean *did* speak to me!"

Mechanically he allowed himself to be led towards the door of the tower which gave entrance to the private way leading to the duchess's room. Bertrand was awaiting him, lantern in hand. Etienne reached the library of the Cardinal d'Herouville, and there he was made to wait with Beauvouloir while Bertrand went on to unlock the other doors, and make sure that the hated son could pass through his father's house without danger. The duke did not awake. Advancing with light steps, Etienne and Beauvouloir heard in that immense chateau no sound but the plaintive groans of the dying woman. Thus the very circumstances attending the birth of Etienne were renewed at the death of his mother. The same tempest, same agony, same dread of awaking the pitiless giant, who, on this occasion at least, slept soundly. Bertrand, as a further precaution, took Etienne in his arms and carried him through the duke's room, intending to give some excuse as to the state of the duchess if the duke awoke and detected him. Etienne's heart was horribly wrung by the same fears which filled the minds of these faithful servants; but this emotion prepared him, in a measure, for the sight that met his eyes in that signorial room, which he had never re-entered since the fatal day when, as a child, the paternal curse had driven him from it.

On the great bed, where happiness never came, he looked for his beloved, and scarcely found her, so emaciated was she. White as her own laces, with scarcely a breath left, she gathered up all her strength to clasp Etienne's hand, and to give him her whole soul, as heretofore, in a look. Chaverny had bequeathed to her all his life in a last farewell. Beauvouloir and Bertrand, the mother and the sleeping duke were all once more assembled. Same place, same scene, same actors! but this was funereal grief in place of the joys of motherhood; the night of death instead of the dawn of life. At that moment the storm, threatened by the melancholy moaning of the sea since sundown, suddenly burst forth.

"Dear flower of my life!" said the mother, kissing her son. "You were taken from my bosom in the midst of a tempest, and in a tempest I am taken from you. Between these storms all life has been stormy to me, except the hours I have spent with you. This is my last joy, mingled with my last pangs. Adieu, my only love! adieu, dear image of two souls that will soon be reunited! Adieu, my only joy - pure joy! adieu, my own beloved!"

"Let me follow thee!" cried Etienne.

"It would be your better fate!" she said, two tears rolling down her livid cheeks; for, as in former days, her eyes seemed to read the future. "Did any one see him?" she asked of the two men.

At this instant the duke turned in his bed; they all trembled.

"Even my last joy is mingled with pain," murmured the duchess. "Take him away! take him away!"

"Mother, I would rather see you a moment longer and die!" said the poor lad, as he fainted by her side.

At a sign from the duchess, Bertrand took Etienne in his arms, and, showing him for the last time to his mother, who kissed him with a last look, he turned to carry him away, awaiting the final order of the dying mother.

"Love him well!" she said to the physician and Bertrand; "he has no protectors but you and Heaven."

Prompted by an instinct which never misleads a mother, she had felt the pity of the old retainer for the eldest son of a house, for which his veneration was only comparable to that of the Jews for their Holy City, Jerusalem. As for Beauvouloir, the compact between himself and the duchess had long been signed. The two servitors, deeply moved to see their mistress forced to bequeath her noble child to none but themselves, promised by a solemn gesture to be the providence of their young master, and the mother had faith in that gesture.

The duchess died towards morning, mourned by the

servants of the household, who, for all comment, were heard to say beside her grave, "She was a comely woman, sent from Paradise."

Etienne's sorrow was the most intense, the most lasting of sorrows, and wholly silent. He wandered no more among his rocks; he felt no strength to read or sing. He spent whole days crouched in the crevice of a rock, caring nought for the inclemency of the weather, motionless, fastened to the granite like the lichen that grew upon it; weeping seldom, lost in one sole thought, immense, infinite as the ocean, and, like that ocean, taking a thousand forms, - terrible, tempestuous, tender, calm. It was more than sorrow; it was a new existence, an irrevocable destiny, dooming this innocent creature to smile no more. There are pangs which, like a drop of blood cast into flowing water, stain the whole current instantly. The stream, renewed from its source, restores the purity of its surface; but with Etienne the source itself was polluted, and each new current brought its own gall.

Bertrand, in his old age, had retained the super-intendence of the stables, so as not to lose the habit of authority in the household. His house was not far from that of Etienne, so that he was ever at hand to watch over the youth with the persistent affection and simple wiliness characteristic of old soldiers. He checked his roughness when speaking to the poor lad; softly he walked in rainy weather to fetch him from his reverie in his crevice to the house. He put his pride into filling the mother's place, so that her child might find, if not her love, at least the same attentions. This pity resembled tenderness. Etienne bore, without complaint or resistance, these attentions of the old retainer, but too many links were now broken between the hated child and other creatures to admit of any keen affection at present in his heart. Mechanically he allowed himself to be protected; he became, as it were, an intermediary creature between man and plant, or, perhaps one might say, between man and God. To what shall we compare a being to whom all social laws, all the false sentiments of the world were unknown, and who kept his ravishing innocence by obeying nought but the instincts of his heart?

Nevertheless, in spite of his sombre melancholy, he came to feel the need of loving, of finding another mother, another soul for his soul. But, separated from civilization by an iron wall, it was well-nigh impossible to meet with a being who had flowered like himself. Instinctively seeking another self to whom to confide his thoughts and whose life might blend with his life, he ended in sympathizing with his Ocean. The sea became to him a living, thinking being. Always in presence of that vast creation, the hidden marvels of which contrast so grandly with those of earth, he discovered the meaning of many mysteries. Familiar from his cradle with the infinitude of those liquid fields, the sea and the sky taught him many poems. To him, all was variety in that vast picture so monotonous to some. Like other men whose souls dominate their bodies, he had a piercing sight which could reach to enormous distances and seize, with admirable ease and without fatigue, the fleeting tints of the clouds, the passing shimmer of the waters. On days of perfect stillness his eyes could see the manifold tints of the ocean, which to him, like the face of a woman, had its physiognomy, its smiles, ideas, caprices; there green and sombre; here smiling and azure; sometimes uniting its brilliant lines with the hazy gleams of the horizon, or again, softly swaying beneath the orange-tinted

heavens. For him all-glorious fetes were celebrated at
sundown when the star of day poured its red colors on
the waves in a crimson flood. For him the sea was gay
and sparkling and spirited when it quivered in
repeating the noonday light from a thousand dazzling
facets; to him it revealed its wondrous melancholy; it
made him weep whenever, calm or sad, it reflected the
dun-gray sky surcharged with clouds. He had learned
the mute language of that vast creation. The flux and
reflux of its waters were to him a melodious breathing
which uttered in his ear a sentiment; he felt and
comprehended its inward meaning. No mariner, no
man of science, could have predicted better than he the
slightest wrath of the ocean, the faintest change on that
vast face. By the manner of the waves as they rose and
died away upon the shore, he could foresee tempests,
surges, squalls, the height of tides, or calms. When
night had spread its veil upon the sky, he still could see
the sea in its twilight mystery, and talk with it. At all
times he shared its fecund life, feeling in his soul the
tempest when it was angry; breathing its rage in its
hissing breath; running with its waves as they broke in
a thousand liquid fringes upon the rocks. He felt
himself intrepid, free, and terrible as the sea itself; like
it, he bounded and fell back; he kept its solemn silence;
he copied its sudden pause. In short, he had wedded
the sea; it was now his confidant, his friend. In the
morning when he crossed the glowing sands of the
beach and came upon his rocks, he divined the temper
of the ocean from a single glance; he could see
landscapes on its surface; he hovered above the face of
the waters, like an angel coming down from heaven.
When the joyous, mischievous white mists cast their
gossamer before him, like a veil before the face of a
bride, he followed their undulations and caprices with
the joy of a lover. His thought, married with that grand

expression of the divine thought, consoled him in his solitude, and the thousand outlooks of his soul peopled its desert with glorious fantasies. He ended at last by divining in the motions of the sea its close communion with the celestial system; he perceived nature in its harmonious whole, from the blade of grass to the wandering stars which seek, like seeds driven by the wind, to plant themselves in ether.

Pure as an angel, virgin of those ideas which degrade mankind, naïve as a child, he lived like a sea-bird, a gull, or a flower, prodigal of the treasures of poetic imagination, and possessed of a divine knowledge, the fruitful extent of which he contemplated in solitude. Incredible mingling of two creations! sometimes he rose to God in prayer; sometimes he descended, humble and resigned, to the quiet happiness of animals. To him the stars were the flowers of night, the birds his friends, the sun was a father. Everywhere he found the soul of his mother; often he saw her in the clouds; he spoke to her; they communicated, veritably, by celestial visions; on certain days he could hear her voice and see her smile; in short, there were days when he had not lost her. God seemed to have given him the power of the hermits of old, to have endowed him with some perfected inner senses which penetrated to the spirit of all things. Unknown moral forces enabled him to go farther than other men into the secrets of the Immortal labor. His yearnings, his sorrows were the links that united him to the unseen world; he went there, armed with his love, to seek his mother; realizing thus, with the sublime harmonies of ecstasy, the symbolic enterprise of Orpheus.

Often, when crouching in the crevice of some rock, capriciously curled up in his granite grotto, the entrance to which was as narrow as that of a charcoal kiln, he would sink into involuntary sleep, his figure softly lighted by the warm rays of the sun which crept through the fissures and fell upon the dainty seaweeds that adorned his retreat, the veritable nest of a sea-bird. The sun, his sovereign lord, alone told him that he had slept, by measuring the time he had been absent from his watery landscapes, his golden sands, his shells and pebbles. Across a light as brilliant as that from heaven he saw the cities of which he read; he looked with amazement, but without envy, at courts and kings, battles, men, and buildings. These daylight dreams made dearer to him his precious flowers, his clouds, his sun, his granite rocks. To attach him the more to his solitary existence, an angel seemed to reveal to him the abysses of the moral world and the terrible shocks of civilization. He felt that his soul, if torn by the throng of men, would perish like a pearl dropped from the crown of a princess into mud.

PART II

HOW THE SON DIED

CHAPTER IV

THE HEIR

In 1617, twenty and some years after the horrible night during which Etienne came into the world, the Duc d'Herouville, then seventy-six years old, broken, decrepit, almost dead, was sitting at sunset in an immense arm-chair, before the gothic window of his bedroom, at the place where his wife had so vainly implored, by the sounds of the horn wasted on the air, the help of men and heaven. You might have thought him a body resurrected from the grave. His once energetic face, stripped of its sinister aspect by old age and suffering, was ghastly in color, matching the long meshes of white hair which fell around his bald head, the yellow skull of which seemed softening. The warrior and the fanatic still shone in those yellow eyes, tempered now by religious sentiment. Devotion had cast a monastic tone upon the face, formerly so hard, but now marked with tints which softened its expression. The reflections of the setting sun colored with a faintly ruddy tinge the head, which, in spite of all infirmities, was still vigorous. The feeble body, wrapped in brown garments, gave, by its heavy attitude and the absence of all movement, a vivid impression of the monotonous existence, the terrible repose of this man once so active, so enterprising, so vindictive.

"Enough!" he said to his chaplain.

That venerable old man was reading aloud the Gospel, standing before the master in a respectful attitude. The duke, like an old menagerie lion which has reached a decrepitude that is still full of majesty, turned to another white-haired man and said, holding out a fleshless arm covered with sparse hairs, still sinewy, but without vigor: -

"Your turn now, bonesetter. How am I to-day?"

"Doing well, monseigneur; the fever has ceased. You will live many years yet."

"I wish I could see Maximilien here," continued the duke, with a smile of satisfaction. "My fine boy! He commands a company in the King's Guard. The Marechal d'Ancre takes care of my lad, and our gracious Queen Marie thinks of allying him nobly, now that he is created Duc de Nivron. My race will be worthily continued. The lad performed prodigies of valor in the attack on -"

At this moment Bertrand entered, holding a letter in his hand.

"What is this?" said the old lord, eagerly.

"A despatch brought by a courier sent to you by the king," replied Bertrand.

"The king, and not the queen-mother!" exclaimed the duke. "What is happening? Have the Huguenots taken arms again? Tete-Dieu!" cried the old man, rising to his feet and casting a flaming glance at his three companions, "I'll arm my soldiers once more, and, with Maximilien at my side, Normandy shall -"

"Sit down, my good seigneur," said Beauvouloir, uneasy at seeing the duke give way to an excitement that was dangerous to a convalescent.

"Read it, Maitre Corbineau," said the old man, holding out the missive to his confessor.

These four personages formed a tableau full of instruction upon human life. The man-at-arms, the priest, and the physician, all three standing before their master, who was seated in his arm-chair, were casting pallid glances about them, each presenting one of those ideas which end by possessing the whole man on the verge of the tomb. Strongly illumined by a last ray of the setting sun, these silent men composed a picture of aged melancholy fertile in contrasts. The sombre and solemn chamber, where nothing had been changed in twenty-five years, made a frame for this poetic canvas, full of extinguished passions, saddened by death, tinctured by religion.

"The Marechal d'Ancre has been killed on the Pont du Louvre by order of the king, and - O God!"

"Go on!" cried the duke.

"Monsieur le Duc de Nivron -"

"Well?"

"Is dead!"

The duke dropped his head upon his breast with a great sigh, but was silent. At those words, at that sigh, the three old men looked at each other. It seemed to them as though the illustrious and opulent house of Herouville was disappearing before their eyes like a sinking ship.

"The Master above," said the duke, casting a terrible glance at the heavens, "is ungrateful to me. He forgets the great deeds I have performed for his holy cause."

"God has avenged himself!" said the priest, in a solemn voice.

"Put that man in the dungeon!" cried the duke.

"You can silence me far more easily than you can your conscience."

The duke sank back in thought.

"My house to perish! My name to be extinct! I will marry! I will have a son!" he said, after a long pause.

Though the expression of despair on the duke's face was truly awful, the bonesetter could not repress a smile. At that instant a song, fresh as the evening breeze, pure as the sky, equable as the color of the ocean, rose above the murmur of the waves, to cast its charm over Nature herself. The melancholy of that voice, the melody of its tones shed, as it were, a perfume rising to the soul; its harmony rose like a vapor filling the air; it poured a balm on sorrows, or rather it consoled them by expressing them. The voice mingled with the gurgle of the waves so perfectly that it seemed to rise from the bosom of the waters. That song was sweeter to the ears of those old men than the tenderest word of love on the lips of a young girl; it brought religious hope into their souls like a voice from heaven.

"What is that?" asked the duke.

"The little nightingale is singing," said Bertrand; "all is not lost, either for him or for us."

"What do you call a nightingale?"

"That is the name we have given to monseigneur's eldest son," replied Bertrand.

"My son!" cried the old man; "have I a son? - a son to bear my name and to perpetuate it!"

He rose to his feet and began to walk about the room with steps in turn precipitate and slow. Then he made an imperious gesture, sending every one away from him except the priest.

The next morning the duke, leaning on the arm of his old retainer Bertrand, walked along the shore and among the rocks looking for the son he had so long hated. He saw him from afar in a recess of the granite rocks, lying carelessly extended in the sun, his head on a tuft of mossy grass, his feet gracefully drawn up beneath him. So lying, Etienne was like a swallow at rest. As soon as the tall old man appeared upon the beach, the sound of his steps mingling faintly with the voice of the waves, the young man turned his head, gave the cry of a startled bird, and disappeared as if into the rock itself, like a mouse darting so quickly into its hole that we doubt if we have even seen it.

"Hey! tete-Dieu! where has he hid himself?" cried the duke, reaching the rock beside which his son had been lying.

"He is there," replied Bertrand, pointing to a narrow crevice, the edges of which had been polished smooth by the repeated assaults of the high tide.

"Etienne, my beloved son!" called the old man.

The hated child made no reply. For hours the duke entreated, threatened, implored in turn, receiving no response. Sometimes he was silent, with his ear at the cleft of the rock, where even his enfeebled hearing could detect the beating of Etienne's heart, the quick pulsations of which echoed from the sonorous roof of his rocky hiding-place.

"At least *he* lives!" said the old man, in a heartrending voice.

Towards the middle of the day, the father, reduced to despair, had recourse to prayer: -

"Etienne," he said, "my dear Etienne, God has punished me for disowning you. He has deprived me of your brother. To-day you are my only child. I love you more than I love myself. I see the wrong I have done; I know that you have in your veins my blood with that of your mother, whose misery was my doing. Come to me; I will try to make you forget my cruelty; I will cherish you for all that I have lost. Etienne, you are the Duc de Nivron, and you will be, after me, the

Duc d'Herouville, peer of France, knight of the Orders and of the Golden Fleece, captain of a hundred men-at-arms, grand-bailiff of Bessin, Governor of Normandy, lord of twenty-seven domains counting sixty-nine steeples, Marquis de Saint-Sever. You shall take to wife the daughter of a prince. Would you have me die of grief? Come! come to me! or here I kneel until I see you. Your old father prays you, he humbles himself before his child as before God himself."

The hated son paid no heed to this language bristling with social ideas and vanities he did not comprehend; his soul remained under the impressions of unconquerable terror. He was silent, suffering great agony. Towards evening the old seigneur, after exhausting all formulas of language, all resources of entreaty, all repentant promises, was overcome by a sort of religious contrition. He knelt down upon the sand and made a vow: -

"I swear to build a chapel to Saint-Jean and Saint-Etienne, the patrons of my wife and son, and to found one hundred masses in honor of the Virgin, if God and the saints will restore to me the affection of my son, the Duc de Nivron, here present."

He remained on his knees in deep humility with clasped hands, praying. Finding that his son, the hope of his name, still did not come to him, great tears rose in his eyes, dry so long, and rolled down his withered cheeks. At this moment, Etienne, hearing no further sounds, glided to the opening of his grotto like a young adder craving the sun. He saw the tears of the stricken old man, he recognized the signs of a true grief, and, seizing his father's hand, he kissed him, saying in the voice of an angel: -

Honore de Balzac

"Oh, mother! forgive me!"

In the fever of his happiness the old duke lifted his feeble offspring in his arms and carried him, trembling like an abducted girl, toward the castle. As he felt the palpitation of his son's body he strove to reassure him, kissing him with all the caution he might have shown in touching a delicate flower; and speaking in the gentlest tones he had ever in his life used, in order to soothe him.

"God's truth! you are like my poor Jeanne, dear child!" he said. "Teach me what would give you pleasure, and I will give you all you can desire. Grow strong! be well! I will show you how to ride a mare as pretty and gentle as yourself. Nothing shall ever thwart or trouble you. Tete-Dieu! all things bow to me as the reeds to the wind. I give you unlimited power. I bow to you myself as the god of the family."

The father carried his son into the lordly chamber where the mother's sad existence had been spent. Etienne turned away and leaned against the window from which his mother was wont to make him signals announcing the departure of his persecutor, who now, without his knowing why, had become his slave, like those gigantic genii which the power of a fairy places at the order of a young prince. That fairy was Feudality. Beholding once more the melancholy room where his eyes were accustomed to contemplate the ocean, tears came into those eyes; recollections of his long misery, mingled with melodious memories of the pleasures he had had in the only love that was granted to him, maternal love, all rushed together upon his heart and developed there, like a poem at once terrible and delicious. The emotions of this youth, accustomed to live in contemplations of ecstasy as others in the excitements of the world, resembled none of the habitual emotions of mankind.

"Will he live?" said the old man, amazed at the fragility of his heir, and holding his breath as he leaned over him.

"I can live only here," replied Etienne, who had heard him, simply.

"Well, then, this room shall be yours, my child."

"What is that noise?" asked the young man, hearing the retainers of the castle who were gathering in the guard-room, whither the duke had summoned them to present his son.

"Come!" said the father, taking him by the hand and leading him into the great hall.

At this epoch of our history, a duke and peer, with great possessions, holding public offices and the government of a province, lived the life of a prince; the cadets of his family did not revolt at serving him. He had his household guard and officers; the first lieutenant of his ordnance company was to him what, in our day, an aide-de-camp is to a marshal. A few years later, Cardinal de Richelieu had his body-guard. Several princes allied to the royal house - Guise, Conde, Nevers, and Vendome, etc. - had pages chosen among the sons of the best families, - a last lingering custom of departed chivalry. The wealth of the Duc d'Herouville, and the antiquity of his Norman race indicated by his name ("herus villoe"), permitted him to imitate the magnificence of families who were in other respects his inferiors, - those, for instance, of Epernon, Luynes, Balagny, d'O, Zamet, regarded as parvenus, but living, nevertheless, as princes. It was therefore an imposing spectacle for poor Etienne to see the assemblage of retainers of all kinds attached to the service of his father.

The duke seated himself on a chair of state placed under a "solium," or dais of carved word, above a platform raised by several steps, from which, in certain provinces, the great seigneurs still delivered judgment on their vassals, - a vestige of feudality which disappeared under the reign of Richelieu. These thrones, like the warden's benches of the churches, have now become objects of collection as curiosities. When Etienne was placed beside his father on that raised platform, he shuddered at feeling himself the centre to which all eyes turned.

"Do not tremble," said the duke, bending his bald head to his son's ear; "these people are only our servants."

Through the dusky light produced by the setting sun, the rays of which were reddening the leaded panes of the windows, Etienne saw the bailiff, the captain and lieutenant of the guard, with certain of their men-at-arms, the chaplain, the secretaries, the doctor, the majordomo, the ushers, the steward, the huntsmen, the game-keeper, the grooms, and the valets. Though all these people stood in respectful attitudes, induced by the terror the old man inspired in even the most important persons under his command, a low murmur, caused by curiosity and expectation, made itself heard. That sound oppressed the bosom of the young man, who felt for the first time in his life the influence of the heavy atmosphere produced by the breath of many persons in a closed hall. His senses, accustomed to the pure and wholesome air from the sea, were shocked with a rapidity that proved the super-sensitiveness of his organs. A horrible palpitation, due no doubt to some defect in the organization of his heart, shook him with reiterated blows when his father, showing himself to the assemblage like some majestic old lion, pronounced in a solemn voice the following brief address: -

"My friends, this is my son Etienne, my first-born son, my heir presumptive, the Duc de Nivron, to whom the king will no doubt grant the honors of his deceased brother. I present him to you that you may acknowledge him and obey him as myself. I warn you that if you, or any one in this province, over which I am governor, does aught to displease the young duke, or thwart him in any way whatsoever, it would be better, should it come to my knowledge, that that man had never been born. You hear me. Return now to your duties, and God guide you. The obsequies of my son Maximilien will take place here when his body arrives. The household will go into mourning eight days hence. Later, we shall celebrate the accession of my son Etienne here present."

"Vive monseigneur! Long live the race of Herouville!" cried the people in a roar that shook the castle.

The valets brought in torches to illuminate the hall. That hurrah, the sudden lights, the sensations caused by his father's speech, joined to those he was already feeling, overcame the young man, who fainted completely and fell into a chair, leaving his slender womanly hand in the broad palm of his father. As the duke, who had signed to the lieutenant of his company to come nearer, saying to him, "I am fortunate, Baron

Honore de Balzac

d'Artagnon, in being able to repair my loss; behold my son!" he felt an icy hand in his. Turning round, he looked at the new Duc de Nivron, and, thinking him dead, he uttered a cry of horror which appalled the assemblage.

Beauvouloir rushed to the platform, took the young man in his arms, and carried him away, saying to his master, "You have killed him by not preparing him for this ceremony."

"He can never have a child if he is like that!" cried the duke, following Beauvouloir into the seignorial chamber, where the doctor laid the young heir upon the bed.

"Well, what think you?" asked the duke presently.

"It is not serious," replied the old physician, showing Etienne, who was now revived by a cordial, a few drops of which he had given him on a bit of sugar, a new and precious substance which the apothecaries were selling for its weight in gold.

"Take this, old rascal!" said the duke, offering his purse to Beauvouloir, "and treat him like the son of a king! If he dies by your fault, I'll burn you myself on a gridiron."

"If you continue to be so violent, the Duc de Nivron will die by your own act," said the doctor, roughly. "Leave him now; he will go to sleep."

"Good-night, my love," said the old man, kissing his son upon the forehead.

"Good-night, father," replied the youth, whose voice made the father - thus named by Etienne for the first time - quiver.

The duke took Beauvouloir by the arm and led him to the next room, where, having pushed him into the recess of a window, he said: -

"Ah ca! old rascal, now we will understand each other."

That term, a favorite sign of graciousness with the duke, made the doctor, no longer a mere bonesetter, smile.

"You know," said the duke, continuing, "that I wish you no harm. You have twice delivered my poor Jeanne, you cured my son Maximilien of an illness, in short, you are a part of my household. Poor Maximilien! I will avenge him; I take upon myself to kill the man who killed him. The whole future of the house of Herouville is now in your hands. You alone can know if there is in that poor abortion the stuff that can breed a Herouville. You hear me. What think you?"

"His life on the seashore has been so chaste and so pure that nature is sounder in him than it would have been had he lived in your world. But so delicate a body is the very humble servant of the soul. Monseigneur Etienne must himself choose his wife; all things in him must be the work of nature and not of your will. He will love artlessly, and will accomplish by his heart's desire that which you wish him to do for the sake of your name. But if you give your son a proud, ungainly woman of the world, a great lady, he will flee to his rocks. More than that; though sudden terror would surely kill him, I believe that any sudden emotion would be equally fatal. My advice therefore is to leave Etienne to choose for himself, at his own pleasure, the path of love. Listen to me, monseigneur; you are a great and powerful prince, but you understand nothing of such matters. Give me your entire confidence, your unlimited confidence, and you shall have a grandson."

"If I obtain a grandson by any sorcery whatever, I shall have you ennobled. Yes, difficult as it may be, I'll make an old rascal into a man of honor; you shall be Baron de Forcalier. Employ your magic, white or black, appeal to your witches' sabbath or the novenas of the Church; what care I how 'tis done, provided my line male continues?"

"I know," said Beauvouloir, "a whole chapter of sorcerers capable of destroying your hopes; they are none other than *yourself*, monseigneur. I know you. To-day you want male lineage at any price; to-morrow you will seek to have it on your own conditions; you will torment your son."

"God preserve me from it!"

"Well, then, go away from here; go to court, where the death of the marechal and the emancipation of the king must have turned everything topsy turvy, and where you certainly have business, if only to obtain the marshal's baton which was promised to you. Leave Monseigneur Etienne to me. But give me your word of honor as a gentleman to approve whatever I may do for him."

The duke struck his hand into that of his physician as a

sign of complete acceptance, and retired to his own apartments.

When the days of a high and mighty seigneur are numbered, the physician becomes a personage of importance in the household. It is, therefore, not surprising to see a former bonesetter so familiar with the Duc d'Herouville. Apart from the illegitimate ties which connected him, by marriage, to this great family and certainly militated in his favor, his sound good sense had so often been proved by the duke that the old man had now become his master's most valued counsellor. Beauvouloir was the Coyctier of this Louis XI. Nevertheless, and no matter how valuable his knowledge might be, he never obtained over the government of Normandy, in whom was the ferocity of religious warfare, as much influence as feudality exercised over that rugged nature. For this reason the physician was confident that the prejudices of the noble would thwart the desires and the vows of the father.

CHAPTER V

GABRIELLE

Great physician that he was, Beauvouloir saw plainly that to a being so delicately organized as Etienne marriage must come as a slow and gentle inspiration, communicating new powers to his being and vivifying it with the fires of love. As he had said to the father, to impose a wife on Etienne would be to kill him. Above all it was important that the young recluse should not be alarmed at the thought of marriage, of which he knew nothing, or be made aware of the object of his father's wishes. This unknown poet conceived as yet only the beautiful and noble passion of Petrarch for Laura, of Dante for Beatrice. Like his mother he was all pure love and soul; the opportunity to love must be given to him, and then the event should be awaited, not compelled. A command to love would have dried within him the very sources of his life.

Maitre Antoine Beauvouloir was a father; he had a daughter brought up under conditions which made her the wife for Etienne. It was so difficult to foresee the events which would make a son, disowned by his father and destined to the priesthood, the presumptive heir of the house of Herouville that Beauvouloir had never until now noticed the resemblance between the fate of Etienne and that of Gabrielle. A sudden idea which now came to him was inspired more by his devotion to those two beings than by ambition.

His wife, in spite of his great skill, had died in child-bed leaving him a daughter whose health was so frail that it seemed as if the mother had bequeathed to her fruit the germs of death. Beauvouloir loved his Gabrielle as old men love their only child. His science and his incessant care had given factitious life to this frail creature, which he cultivated as a florist cultivates an exotic plant. He had kept her hidden from all eyes on his estate of Forcalier, where she was protected against the dangers of the time by the general good-will felt for a man to whom all owed gratitude, and whose scientific powers inspired in the ignorant minds of the country-people a superstitious awe.

By attaching himself to the house of Herouville, Beauvouloir had increased still further the immunity he enjoyed in the province, and had thwarted all attempts of his enemies by means of his powerful influence with the governor. He had taken care, however, in coming to reside at the castle, not to bring with him the flower he cherished in secret at Forcalier, a domain more important for its landed value than for the house then upon it, but with which he expected to obtain for his daughter an establishment in conformity with his views. While promising the duke a posterity and requiring his master's word of honor to approve his acts, he thought suddenly of Gabrielle, of that sweet child whose mother had been neglected and forgotten by the duke as he had also neglected and forgotten his son Etienne.

He awaited the departure of his master before putting his plan into execution; foreseeing that, if the duke became aware of it, the enormous difficulties in the way would be from the first insurmountable.

Beauvouloir's house at Forcalier had a southern exposure on the slope of one of those gentle hills which surround the vales of Normandy; a thick wood shielded it from the north; high walls and Norman hedges and deep ditches made the enclosure inviolable. The garden, descending by an easy incline to the river which watered the valley, had a thick double hedge at its foot, forming an natural embankment. Within this double hedge wound a hidden path, led by the sinuosities of the stream, which the willows, oaks, and beeches made as leafy as a woodland glade. From the house to this natural rampart stretched a mass of verdure peculiar to that rich soil; a beautiful green sheet bordered by a fringe of rare trees, the tones of which formed a tapestry of exquisite coloring: there, the silvery tints of a pine stood forth against the darker green of several alders; here, before a group of sturdy oaks a slender poplar lifted its palm-like figure, ever swaying; farther on, the weeping willows drooped their pale foliage between the stout, round-headed walnuts. This belt of trees enabled the occupants of the house to go down at all hours to the river-bank fearless of the rays of the sun.

The facade of the house, before which lay the yellow ribbon of a gravelled terrace, was shaded by a wooden gallery, around which climbing plants were twining, and tossing in this month of May their various blossoms into the very windows of the second floor. Without being really vast, this garden seemed immense from the manner in which its vistas were cut; points of view, cleverly contrived through the rise and fall of the ground, married themselves, as it were, to those of the valley, where the eye could rove at will. Following the instincts of her thought, Gabrielle could either enter the solitude of a narrow space, seeing naught but the thick green and the blue of the sky above the tree-tops, or she could hover above a glorious prospect, letting her eyes follow those many-shaded green lines, from the brilliant colors of the foreground to the pure tones of the horizon on which they lost themselves, sometimes in the blue ocean of the atmosphere, sometimes in the cumuli that floated above it.

Watched over by her grandmother and served by her former nurse, Gabrielle Beauvouloir never left this modest home except for the parish church, the steeple of which could be seen at the summit of the hill, whither she was always accompanied by her grand-mother, her nurse, and her father's valet. She had reached the age of seventeen in that sweet ignorance which the rarity of books allowed a girl to retain without appearing extraordinary at a period when educated women were thought phenomenal. The house had been to her a convent, but with more freedom, less enforced prayer, - a retreat where she had lived beneath the eye of a pious old woman and the protection of her father, the only man she had ever known. This absolute solitude, necessitated from her birth by the apparent feebleness of her constitution, had been carefully maintained by Beauvouloir.

As Gabrielle grew up, such constant care and the purity of the atmosphere had gradually strengthened her fragile youth. Still, the wise physician did not deceive himself when he saw the pearly tints around his daughter's eyes soften or darken or flush according to the emotions that overcame her; the weakness of the body and the strength of the soul were made plain to

Honore de Balzac

him in that one indication which his long experience enabled him to understand. Besides this, Gabrielle's celestial beauty made him fearful of attempts too common in times of violence and sedition. Many reasons had thus induced the good father to deepen the shadows and increase the solitude that surrounded his daughter, whose excessive sensibility alarmed him; a passion, an assault, a shock of any kind might wound her mortally. Though she seldom deserved blame, a mere word of reproach overcame her; she kept it in the depths of her heart, where it fostered a meditative melancholy; she would turn away weeping, and wept long.

Thus the moral education of the young girl required no less care than her physical education. The old physician had been compelled to cease telling stories, such as all children love, to his daughter; the impressions she received were too vivid. Wise through long practice, he endeavored to develop her body in order to deaden the blows which a soul so powerful gave to it. Gabrielle was all of life and love to her father, his only heir, and never had he hesitated to procure for her such things as might produce the results he aimed for. He carefully removed from her knowledge books, pictures, music, all those creations of art which awaken thought. Aided by his mother he interested Gabrielle in manual exercises. Tapestry, sewing, lace-making, the culture of flowers, household cares, the storage of fruits, in short, the most material occupations of life, were the food given to the mind of this charming creature. Beauvouloir brought her beautiful spinning-wheels, finely-carved chests, rich carpets, pottery of Bernard de Palissy, tables, prie-dieus, chairs beautifully wrought and covered with precious stuffs, embroidered line and jewels. With an instinct given by paternity, the old man always chose his presents among the works of that fantastic order called arabesque, which, speaking neither to the soul nor the senses, addresses the mind only by its creations of pure fantasy.

Thus - singular to say! - the life which the hatred of a father had imposed on Etienne d'Herouville, paternal love had induced Beauvouloir to impose on Gabrielle. In both these children the soul was killing the body; and without an absolute solitude, ordained by cruelty for one and procured by science for the other, each was likely to succumb, - he to terror, she beneath the weight of a too keen emotion of love. But, alas! instead of being born in a region of gorse and moor, in the midst of an arid nature of hard and angular shapes, such as all great painters have given as backgrounds to their Virgins, Gabrielle lived in a rich and fertile valley. Beauvouloir could not destroy the harmonious grouping of the native woods, the graceful upspringing of the wild flowers, the cool softness of the grassy slopes, the love expressed in the intertwining growth of the clustering plants. Such ever-living poesies have a language heard, rather than understood by the poor girl, who yielded to vague misery among the shadows. Across the misty ideas suggested by her long study of this beautiful landscape, observed at all seasons and through all the variations of a marine atmosphere in which the fogs of England come to die and the sunshine of France is born, there rose within her soul a distant light, a dawn which pierced the darkness in which her father kept her.

Beauvouloir had never withdrawn his daughter from the influence of Divine love; to a deep admiration of nature she joined her girlish adoration of the Creator,

Honore de Balzac

springing thus into the first way open to the feelings of womanhood. She loved God, she loved Jesus, the Virgin and the saints; she loved the Church and its pomps; she was Catholic after the manner of Saint Teresa, who saw in Jesus an eternal spouse, a continual marriage. Gabrielle gave herself up to this passion of strong souls with so touching a simplicity that she would have disarmed the most brutal seducer by the infantine naivete of her language.

Whither was this life of innocence leading Gabrielle? How teach a mind as pure as the water of a tranquil lake, reflecting only the azure of the skies? What images should be drawn upon that spotless canvas? Around which tree must the tendrils of this bind-weed twine? No father has ever put these questions to himself without an inward shudder.

At this moment the good old man of science was riding slowly on his mule along the roads from Herouville to Ourscamp (the name of the village near which the estate of Forcalier was situated) as if he wished to keep that way unending. The infinite love he bore his daughter suggested a bold project to his mind. One only being in all the world could make her happy; that man was Etienne. Assuredly, the angelic son of Jeanne de Saint-Savin and the guileless daughter of Gertrude Marana were twin beings. All other women would frighten and kill the heir of Herouville; and Gabrielle, so Beauvouloir argued, would perish by contact with any man in whom sentiments and external forms had not the virgin delicacy of those of Etienne. Certainly the poor physician had never dreamed of such a result; chance had brought it forward and seemed to ordain it. But, under, the reign of Louis XIII., to dare to lead a Duc d'Herouville to marry the daughter of a bonesetter!

And yet, from this marriage alone was it likely that the lineage imperiously demanded by the old duke would result. Nature had destined these two rare beings for each other; God had brought them together by a marvellous arrangement of events, while, at the same time, human ideas and laws placed insuperable barriers between them. Though the old man thought he saw in this the finger of God, and although he had forced the duke to pass his word, he was seized with such fear, as his thoughts reverted to the violence of that ungovernable nature, that he returned upon his steps when, on reaching the summit of the hill above Ourscamp, he saw the smoke of his own chimneys among the trees that enclosed his home. Then, changing his mind once more, the thought of the illegitimate relationship decided him; that consideration might have great influence on the mind of his master. Once decided, Beauvouloir had confidence in the chances and changes of life; it might be that the duke would die before the marriage; besides, there were many examples of such marriage; a peasant girl in Dauphine, Francoise Mignot, had lately married the Marechal d'Hopital; the son of the Connetable Anne de Montmorency had married Diane, daughter of Henri II. and a Piedmontese lady named Philippa Duc.

During this mental deliberation in which paternal love measured all probabilities and discussed both the good and the evil chances, striving to foresee the future and weighing its elements, Gabrielle was walking in the garden and gathering flowers for the vases of that illustrious potter, who did for glaze what Benvenuto Cellini did for metal. Gabrielle had put one of these vases, decorated with animals in relief, on a table in the middle of the hall, and was filling it with flowers to enliven her grandmother, and also, perhaps, to give form to her own ideas. The noble vase, of the pottery called Limoges, was filled, arranged, and placed upon the handsome table-cloth, and Gabrielle was saying to her grandmother, "See!" when Beauvouloir entered. The young girl ran to her father's arms. After this first outburst of affection she wanted him to admire her bouquet; but the old man, after glancing at it, cast a long, deep look at his daughter, which made her blush.

"The time has come," he said to himself, understanding the language of those flowers, each of which had doubtless been studied as to form and as to color, and given its true place in the bouquet, where it produced its own magical effect.

Gabrielle remained standing, forgetting the flower begun on her tapestry. As he looked at his daughter a tear rolled from Beauvouloir's eyes, furrowed his cheeks which seldom wore a serious aspect, and fell upon his shirt, which, after the fashion of the day, his open doublet exposed to view above his breeches. He threw off his felt hat, adorned with an old red plume, in order to rub his hand over his bald head. Again he looked at his daughter, who, beneath the brown rafters of that leather-hung room, with its ebony furniture and portieres of silken damask, and its tall chimney-piece, the whole so softly lighted, was still his very own. The poor father felt the tears in his eyes and hastened to wipe them. A father who loves his daughter longs to keep her always a child; as for him who can without deep pain see her fall under the dominion of another man, he does not rise to worlds superior, he falls to lowest space.

"What ails you, my son?" said his old mother, taking off her spectacles, and seeking the cause of his silence and of the change in his usually joyous manner.

The old physician signed to the old mother to look at his daughter, nodding his head with satisfaction as if to say, "How sweet she is!"

What father would not have felt Beauvouloir's emotion on seeing the young girl as she stood there in the Norman dress of that period? Gabrielle wore the corset pointed before and square behind, which the Italian masters give almost invariably to their saints and their madonnas. This elegant corselet, made of sky-blue velvet, as dainty as that of a dragon-fly, enclosed the bust like a guimpe and compressed it, delicately modelling the outline as it seemed to flatten; it moulded the shoulders, the back, the waist, with the precision of a drawing made by an able draftsman, ending around the neck in an oblong curve, adorned at the edges with a slight embroidery in brown silks, leaving to view as much of the bare throat as was needed to show the beauty of her womanhood, but not enough to awaken desire. A full brown skirt, continuing the lines already drawn by the velvet waist, fell to her feet in narrow flattened pleats. Her figure was so slender that Gabrielle seemed tall; her arms hung pendent with the inertia that some deep thought imparts to the attitude. Thus standing, she presented a living model of those ingenuous works of statuary a taste for which prevailed at that period, - works which obtained admiration for the harmony of their lines, straight without stiffness, and for the firmness of a design which did not exclude vitality. No swallow, brushing the window-panes at dusk, ever conveyed the idea of greater elegance of outline.

Gabrielle's face was thin, but not flat; on her neck and

Honore de Balzac

forehead ran bluish threads showing the delicacy of a skin so transparent that the flowing of the blood through her veins seemed visible. This excessive whiteness was faintly tinted with rose upon the cheeks. Held beneath a little coif of sky-blue velvet embroidered with pearls, her hair, of an even tone, flowed like two rivulets of gold from her temples and played in ringlets on her neck, which it did not hide. The glowing color of those silky locks brightened the dazzling whiteness of the neck, and purified still further by its reflections the outlines of the face already so pure. The eyes, which were long and as if pressed between their lids, were in harmony with the delicacy of the head and body; their pearl-gray tints were brilliant without vivacity, candid without passion. The line of the nose might have seemed cold, like a steel blade, without two rosy nostrils, the movements of which were out of keeping with the chastity of that dreamy brow, often perplexed, sometimes smiling, but always of an august serenity. An alert little ear attracted the eye, peeping beneath the coif and between two curls, and showing a ruby ear-drop, the color of which stood vigorously out on the milky whiteness of the neck. This was neither Norman beauty, where flesh abounds, nor French beauty, as fugitive as its own expressions, nor the beauty of the North, cold and melancholy as the North itself - it was the deep seraphic beauty of the Catholic Church, supple and rigid, severe but tender.

"Where could one find a prettier duchess?" thought Beauvouloir, contemplating his daughter with delight. As she stood there slightly bending, her neck stretched out to watch the flight of a bird past the windows, he could only compare her to a gazelle pausing to listen for the ripple of the water where she seeks to drink.

"Come and sit here," said Beauvouloir, tapping his knee and making a sign to Gabrielle, which told her he had something to whisper to her.

Gabrielle understood him, and came. She placed herself on his knee with the lightness of a gazelle, and slipped her arm about his neck, ruffling his collar.

"Tell me," he said, "what were you thinking of when you gathered those flowers? You have never before arranged them so charmingly."

"I was thinking of many things," she answered. "Looking at the flowers made for us, I wondered whom we were made for; who are they who look at us? You are wise, and I can tell you what I think; you know so much you can explain all. I feel a sort of force within me that wants to exercise itself; I struggle against something. When the sky is gray I am half content; I am sad, but I am calm. When the day is fine, and the flowers smell sweet, and I sit on my bench down there among the jasmine and honeysuckles, something rises in me, like waves which beat against my stillness. Ideas come into my mind which shake me, and fly away like those birds before the windows; I cannot hold them. Well, when I have made a bouquet in which the colors blend like tapestry, and the red contrasts with white, and the greens and the browns cross each other, when all seems so abundant, the breeze so playful, the flowers so many that their fragrance mingles and their buds interlace, - well, then I am happy, for I see what is passing in me. At church when the organ plays and the clergy respond, there are two distinct songs speaking to each other, - the human voice and the music. Well, then, too, I am happy; that harmony echoes in my breast. I pray with a pleasure which stirs my blood."

While listening to his daughter, Beauvouloir examined her with sagacious eyes; those eyes seemed almost stupid from the force of his rushing thoughts, as the water of a cascade seems motionless. He raised the veil of flesh which hid the secret springs by which the soul reacts upon the body; he studied the diverse symptoms which his long experience had noted in persons committed to his care, and he compared them with those contained in this frail body, the bones of which frightened him by their delicacy, as the milk-white skin alarmed him by its want of substance. He tried to bring the teachings of his science to bear upon the future of that angelic child, and he was dizzy in so doing, as though he stood upon the verge of an abyss; the too vibrant voice, the too slender bosom of the young girl filled him with dread, and he questioned himself after questioning her.

"You suffer here!" he cried at last, driven by a last thought which summed up his whole meditation.

She bent her head gently.

"By God's grace!" said the old man, with a sigh, "I will take you to the Chateau d'Herouville, and there you shall take sea-baths to strengthen you."

"Is that true, father? You are not laughing at your little Gabrielle? I have so longed to see the castle, and the men-at-arms, and the captains of monseigneur."

"Yes, my daughter, you shall really go there. Your nurse and Jean shall accompany you."

"Soon?"

"To-morrow," said the old man, hurrying into the garden to hide his agitation from his mother and his child.

"God is my witness," he cried to himself, "that no ambitious thought impels me. My daughter to save, poor little Etienne to make happy, - those are my only motives."

If he thus interrogated himself it was because, in the depths of his consciousness, he felt an inextinguishable satisfaction in knowing that the success of his project would make Gabrielle some day the Duchesse d'Hero-uville. There is always a man in a father. He walked about a long time, and when he came in to supper he took delight for the rest of the evening in watching his daughter in the midst of the soft brown poesy with which he had surrounded her; and when, before she went to bed, they all - the grandmother, the nurse, the doctor, and Gabrielle - knelt together to say their evening prayer, he added the words, -

"Let us pray to God to bless my enterprise."

The eyes of the grandmother, who knew his intentions, were moistened with what tears remained to her. Gabrielle's face was flushed with happiness. The father trembled, so much did he fear some catastrophe.

"After all," his mother said to him, "fear not, my son. The duke would never kill his grandchild."

"No," he replied, "but he might compel her to marry some brute of a baron, and that would kill her."

The next day Gabrielle, mounted on an ass, followed by her nurse on foot, her father on his mule, and a valet who led two horses laden with baggage, started for the castle of Herouville, where the caravan arrived at nightfall. In order to keep this journey secret, Beauvouloir had taken by-roads, starting early in the morning, and had brought provisions to be eaten by the way, in order not to show himself at hostelries. The party arrived, therefore, after dark, without being noticed by the castle retinue, at the little dwelling on the seashore, so long occupied by the hated son, where Bertrand, the only person the doctor had taken into his confidence, awaited them. The old retainer helped the nurse and valet to unload the horses and carry in the baggage, and otherwise establish the daughter of Beauvouloir in Etienne's former abode. When Bertrand saw Gabrielle, he was amazed.

"I seem to see madame!" he cried. "She is slim and willowy like her; she has madame's coloring and the same fair hair. The old duke will surely love her."

"God grant it!" said Beauvouloir. "But will he acknowledge his own blood after it has passed through mine?"

"He can't deny it," replied Bertrand. "I often went to fetch him from the door of the Belle Romaine, who lived in the rue Culture-Sainte-Catherine. The Cardinal de Lorraine was compelled to give her up to monseigneur, out of shame at being insulted by the mob when he left her house. Monseigneur, who in those days was still in his twenties, will remember that affair; bold he was, - I can tell it now - he led the insulters!"

"He never thinks of the past," said Beauvouloir. "He knows my wife is dead, but I doubt if he remembers I have a daughter."

"Two old navigators like you and me ought to be able to bring the ship to port," said Bertrand. "After all, suppose the duke does get angry and seize our carcasses; they have served their time."

Honore de Balzac

CHAPTER VI

LOVE

Before starting for Paris, the Duc d'Herouville had forbidden the castle servants under heavy pains and penalties to go upon the shore where Etienne had passed his life, unless the Duc de Nivron took any of them with him. This order, suggested by Beauvouloir, who had shown the duke the wisdom of leaving Etienne master of his solitude, guaranteed to Gabrielle and her attendants the inviolability of the little domain, outside of which he forbade them to go without his permission.

Etienne had remained during these two days shut up in the old seignorial bedroom under the spell of his tenderest memories. In that bed his mother had slept; her thoughts had been confided to the furnishings of that room; she had used them; her eyes had often wandered among those draperies; how often she had gone to that window to call with a cry, a sign, her poor disowned child, now master of the chateau. Alone in that room, whither he had last come secretly, brought by Beauvouloir to kiss his dying mother, he fancied that she lived again; he spoke to her, he listened to her, he drank from that spring that never faileth, and from which have flowed so many songs like the "Super flumina Babylonis."

The day after Beauvouloir's return he went to see his young master and blamed him gently for shutting himself up in a single room, pointing out to him the danger of leading a prison life in place of his former free life in the open air.

"But this air is vast," replied Etienne. "The spirit of my mother is in it."

The physician prevailed, however, by the gentle influence of affection, in making Etienne promise that he would go out every day, either on the seashore, or in the fields and meadows which were still unknown to him. In spite of this, Etienne, absorbed in his memories, remained yet another day at his window watching the sea, which offered him from that point of view aspects so various that never, as he believed, had he seen it so beautiful. He mingled his contemplations with readings in Petrarch, one of his most favorite authors, - him whose poesy went nearest to the young man's heart through the constancy and the unity of his love. Etienne had not within him the stuff for several passions. He could love but once, and in one way only. If that love, like all that is a unit, were intense, it must also be calm in its expression, sweet and pure like the sonnets of the Italian poet.

At sunset this child of solitude began to sing, in the marvellous voice which had entered suddenly, like a hope, into the dullest of all ears to music, - those of his father. He expressed his melancholy by varying the same air, which he repeated, again and again, like the nightingale. This air, attributed to the late King Henri IV., was not the so-called air of "Gabrielle," but something far superior as art, as melody, as the expression of infinite tenderness. The admirers of those ancient tunes will recognize the words, composed by the great king to this air, which were taken, probably, from some folk-song to which his cradle had been rocked among the mountains of Bearn.

> "Dawn, approach,
> I pray thee;
> It gladdens me to see thee;
> The maiden
> Whom I love
> Is rosy, rosy like thee;
> The rose itself,
> Dew-laden,
> Has not her freshness;
> Ermine has not
> Her pureness;
> Lilies have not
> Her whiteness."

After naively revealing the thought of his heart in song, Etienne contemplated the sea, saying to himself: "There is my bride; the only love for me!" Then he sang too other lines of the canzonet, -

> "She is fair
> Beyond compare," -

repeating it to express the imploring poesy which abounds in the heart of a timid young man, brave only when alone. Dreams were in that undulating song, sung, resung, interrupted, renewed, and hushed at last in a final modulation, the tones of which died away like the lingering vibrations of a bell.

At this moment a voice, which he fancied was that of a siren rising from the sea, a woman's voice, repeated the air he had sung, but with all the hesitations of a person to whom music is revealed for the first time. He recognized the stammering of a heart born into the poesy of harmony. Etienne, to whom long study of his own voice had taught the language of sounds, in which the soul finds resources greater than speech to express its thoughts, could divine the timid amazement that attended these attempts. With what religious and subtle admiration had that unknown being listened to him! The stillness of the atmosphere enabled him to hear every sound, and he quivered at the distant rustle of the folds of a gown. He was amazed, - he, whom all emotions produced by terror sent to the verge of death - to feel within him the healing, balsamic sensation which his mother's coming had formerly brought to him.

"Come, Gabrielle, my child," said the voice of Beauvouloir, "I forbade you to stay upon the seashore after sundown; you must come in, my daughter."

"Gabrielle," said Etienne to himself. "Oh! the pretty name!"
Beauvouloir presently came to him, rousing his young master from one of those meditations which resemble dreams. It was night, and the moon was rising.

"Monseigneur," said the physician, "you have not been out to-day, and it is not wise of you."

"And I," replied Etienne, "can *I* go on the seashore after sundown?"

The double meaning of this speech, full of the gentle playfulness of a first desire, made the old man smile.

"You have a daughter, Beauvouloir."

"Yes, monseigneur, - the child of my old age; my darling child. Monseigneur, the duke, your father, charged me so earnestly to watch your precious health that, not being able to go to Forcalier, where she was, I have brought her here, to my great regret. In order to conceal her from all eyes, I have placed her in the house monseigneur used to occupy. She is so delicate I fear everything, even a sudden sentiment or emotion. I have never taught her anything; knowledge would kill her."

"She knows nothing!" cried Etienne, surprised.

"She has all the talents of a good housewife, but she has lived as the plants live. Ignorance, monseigneur, is as sacred a thing as knowledge. Knowledge and ignorance are only two ways of living, for the human creature. Both preserve the soul and envelop it; knowledge is your existence, but ignorance will save my daughter's life. Pearls well-hidden escape the diver, and live happy. I can only compare my Gabrielle to a pearl; her skin has the pearl's translucence, her soul its softness, and until this day Forcalier has been her fostering shell."

"Come with me," said Etienne, throwing on a cloak. "I want to walk on the seashore, the air is so soft."

Beauvouloir and his master walked in silence until they reached a spot where a line of light, coming from between the shutters of a fisherman's house, had furrowed the sea with a golden rivulet.

"I know not how to express," said Etienne, addressing his companion, "the sensations that light, cast upon the water, excites in me. I have often watched it streaming from the windows of that room," he added, pointing back to his mother's chamber, "until it was extinguished."

"Delicate as Gabrielle is," said Beauvouloir, gaily, "she can come and walk with us; the night is warm, and the air has no dampness. I will fetch her; but be prudent, monseigneur."

Etienne was too timid to propose to accompany Beauvouloir into the house; besides, he was in that torpid state into which we are plunged by the influx of ideas and sensations which give birth to the dawn of passion. Conscious of more freedom in being alone, he cried out, looking at the sea now gleaming in the moonlight, -

"The Ocean has passed into my soul!"

The sight of the lovely living statuette which was now advancing towards him, silvered by the moon and wrapped in its light, redoubled the palpitations of his heart, but without causing him to suffer.

"My child," said Beauvouloir, "this is monseigneur."

In a moment poor Etienne longed for his father's colossal figure; he would fain have seemed strong, not puny. All the vanities of love and manhood came into his heart like so many arrows, and he remained in gloomy silence, measuring for the first time the extent of his imperfections. Embarrassed by the salutation of the young girl, he returned it awkwardly, and stayed beside Beauvouloir, with whom he talked as they paced along the shore; presently, however, Gabrielle's timid and deprecating countenance emboldened him, and he dared to address her. The incident of the song was the result of mere chance. Beauvouloir had intentionally made no preparations; he thought, wisely, that between two beings in whom solitude had left pure hearts, love would arise in all its simplicity. The repetition of the air by Gabrielle was a ready text on which to begin a conversation.

During this promenade Etienne was conscious of that bodily buoyancy which all men have felt at the moment when a first love transports their vital principle into another being. He offered to teach Gabrielle to sing. The poor lad was so glad to show himself to this young girl invested with some slight superiority that he trembled with pleasure when she accepted his offer. At that moment the moonlight fell full upon her, and enabled Etienne to note the points of her resemblance to his mother, the late duchess. Like Jeanne de Saint-Savin, Beauvouloir's daughter was slender and delicate; in her, as in the duchess, sadness and suffering conveyed a mysterious charm. She had that nobility of manner peculiar to souls on whom the ways of the world have had no influence, and in whom all is noble because all is natural. But in Gabrielle's veins there was also the blood of "la belle Romaine," which had flowed there from two generations, giving to this young girl the passionate heart of a courtesan in an absolutely pure soul; hence the enthusiasm that sometimes reddened her cheek, sanctified her brow, and made her exhale her soul like a flash of light, and communicated the sparkle of flame to all her motions. Beauvouloir shuddered when he noticed this phenomenon, which we may call in these days the phosphorescence of thought; the old physician of that period regarded it as the precursor of death.

Hidden beside her father, Gabrielle endeavored to see Etienne at her ease, and her looks expressed as much curiosity as pleasure, as much kindliness as innocent daring. Etienne detected her in stretching her neck around Beauvouloir with the movement of a timid bird looking out of its nest. To her the young man seemed not feeble, but delicate; she found him so like herself that nothing alarmed her in this sovereign lord. Etienne's sickly complexion, his beautiful hands, his languid smile, his hair parted in the middle into two straight bands, ending in curls on the lace of his large flat collar, his noble brow, furrowed with youthful wrinkles, - all these contrasts of luxury and weakness, power and pettiness, pleased her; perhaps they gratified the instinct of maternal protection, which is the germ of love; perhaps, also, they stimulated the need that every woman feels to find distinctive signs in the man she is prompted to love. New ideas, new sensations were rising in each with a force, with an abundance that enlarged their souls; both remained silent and overcome, for sentiments are least demonstrative when most real and deep. All durable love begins by dreamy meditation. It was suitable that these two beings should first see each other in the softer light of the moon, that love and its splendors might not dazzle them too suddenly; it was well that they met by the shores of the Ocean, - vast image of the vastness of their feelings. They parted filled with one another, fearing, each, to have failed to please.

From his window Etienne watched the lights of the house where Gabrielle was. During that hour of hope mingled with fear, the young poet found fresh meanings in Petrarch's sonnets. He had now seen Laura, a delicate, delightful figure, pure and glowing like a sunray, intelligent as an angel, feeble as a woman. His twenty years of study found their meaning, he understood the mystic marriage of all beauties; he perceived how much of womanhood there was in the poems he adored; in short, he had so long loved unconsciously that his whole past now blended with the emotions of this glorious night. Gabrielle's resemblance to his mother seemed to him an order divinely given. He did not betray his love for the one in loving the other; this new love continued HER maternity. He contemplated that young girl, asleep in the cottage, with the same feelings his mother had felt for him when he was there. Here, again, was a similitude which bound this present to the past. On the clouds of memory the saddened face of his mother appeared to him; he saw once more her feeble smile, he heard her gentle voice; she bowed her head and wept. The lights in the cottage were extinguished. Etienne sang once more the pretty canzonet, with a new expression, a new meaning. From afar Gabrielle again replied. The young girl, too, was making her first voyage into the charmed land of amorous ecstasy. That echoed answer filled with joy the young man's heart; the blood flowing in his veins gave him a strength he never yet had felt, love made him powerful. Feeble beings alone know the voluptuous joy of that new creation entering their life. The poor, the suffering, the ill-used, have joys ineffable; small things to them are worlds. Etienne was bound by many a tie to the dwellers in the City of Sorrows. His recent accession to grandeur had caused him terror only; love now shed within him the balm that created strength; he loved Love.

The next day Etienne rose early to hasten to his old house, where Gabrielle, stirred by curiosity and an impatience she did not acknowledge to herself, had already curled her hair and put on her prettiest costume. Both were full of the eager desire to see each other again, - mutually fearing the results of the interview. As for Etienne, he had chosen his finest lace, his best-embroidered mantle, his violet-velvet breeches; in short, those handsome habiliments which we connect in all memoirs of the time with the pallid face of Louis XIII., a face oppressed with pain in the midst of grandeur, like that of Etienne. Clothes were certainly not the only point of resemblance between the king and the subject. Many other sensibilities were in Etienne as in Louis XIII., - chastity, melancholy, vague but real sufferings, chivalrous timidities, the fear of not being able to express a feeling in all its purity, the dread of too quickly approaching happiness, which all great souls desire to delay, the sense of the burden of power, that tendency to obedience which is found in natures indifferent to material interests, but full of love for what a noble religious genius has called the "astral."

Though wholly inexpert in the ways of the world, Gabrielle was conscious that the daughter of a doctor, the humble inhabitant of Forcalier, was cast at too great a distance from Monseigneur Etienne, Duc de Nivron and heir to the house of Herouville, to allow them to be equal; she had as yet no conception of the ennobling of love. The naive creature thought with no ambition of a place where every other girl would have longed to seat herself; she saw the obstacles only. Loving, without as yet knowing what it was to love, she only felt herself distant from her pleasure, and longed to get nearer to it, as a child longs for the golden grapes hanging high above its head. To a girl whose emotions were stirred at the sight of a flower, and who had unconsciously foreseen love in the chants of the liturgy, how sweet and how strong must have been the feelings inspired in her breast the previous night by the sight of the young seigneur's feebleness, which seemed to reassure her own. But during the night Etienne had been magnified to her mind; she had made him a hope, a power; she had placed him so high that now she despaired of ever reaching him.

"Will you permit me to sometimes enter your domain?" asked the duke, lowing his eyes.

Seeing Etienne so timid, so humble, - for he, on his part, had magnified Beauvouloir's daughter, - Gabrielle was embarrassed with the sceptre he placed in her hands; and yet she was profoundly touched and flattered by such submission. Women alone know what seduction the respect of their master and lover has for them. Nevertheless, she feared to deceive herself, and, curious like the first woman, she wanted to know all.

"I thought you promised yesterday to teach me music," she answered, hoping that music might be made a pretext for their meetings.

If the poor child had known what Etienne's life really was, she would have spared him that doubt. To him his word was the echo of his mind, and Gabrielle's little speech caused him infinite pain. He had come with his heart full, fearing some cloud upon his daylight, and he met a doubt. His joy was extinguished; back into his desert he plunged, no longer finding there the flowers with which he had embellished it. With that prescience of sorrows which characterizes the angel charged to soften them - who is, no doubt, the Charity of heaven - Gabrielle instantly divined the pain she had caused. She was so vividly aware of her fault that she prayed for the power of God to lay bare her soul to Etienne, for she knew the cruel pang a reproach or a stern look was capable of causing; and she artlessly betrayed to him these clouds as they rose in her soul, - the golden swathings of her dawning love. One tear which escaped her eyes turned Etienne's pain to pleasure, and he inwardly accused himself of tyranny. It was fortunate for both that in the very beginning of their love they should thus come to know the diapason of their hearts; they avoided henceforth a thousand shocks which might have wounded them.

Etienne, impatient to entrench himself behind an occupation, led Gabrielle to a table before the little window at which he himself had suffered so long, and where he was henceforth to admire a flower more dainty than all he had hitherto studied. Then he opened a book over which they bent their heads till their hair touched and mingled.

These two beings, so strong in heart, so weak in body, but embellished by all the graces of suffering, were a touching sight. Gabrielle was ignorant of coquetry; a look was given the instant it was asked for, the soft rays from the eyes of each never ceasing to mingle, unless from modesty. The young girl took the joy of telling Etienne what pleasure his voice gave her as she listened to his song; she forgot the meaning of his words when he explained to her the position of the notes or their value; she listened to HIM, leaving melody for the instrument, the idea for the form; ingenuous flattery! the first that true love meets. Gabrielle thought Etienne handsome; she would have liked to stroke the velvet of his mantle, to touch the lace of his broad collar. As for Etienne he was trans-formed under the creative glance of those earnest eyes; they infused

Honore de Balzac

into his being a fruitful sap, which sparkled in his eyes, shone on his brow, remade him inwardly, so that he did not suffer from this new play of his faculties; on the contrary they were strengthened by it. Happiness is the mother's milk of a new life.

As nothing came to distract them from each other, they stayed together not only this day but all days; for they belonged to one another from the first hour, passing the sceptre from one to the other and playing with themselves as children play with life. Sitting, happy and content, upon the golden sands, they told each other their past, painful for him, but rich in dreams; dreamy for her, but full of painful pleasure.

"I never had a mother," said Gabrielle, "but my father has been good as God himself."

"I never had a father," said the hated son, "but my mother was all of heaven to me."

Etienne related his youth, his love for his mother, his taste for flowers. Gabrielle exclaimed at his last words. Questioned why, she blushed and avoided answering; then when a shadow passed across that brow which death seemed to graze with its pinion, across that visible soul where the young man's slightest emotions showed, she answered: -

"Because I too love flowers."

To believe ourselves linked far back in the past by community of tastes, is not that a declaration of love such as virgins know how to give? Love desires to seem old; it is a coquetry of youth.

Etienne brought flowers on the morrow, ordering his people to find rare ones, as his mother had done in earlier days for him. Who knows the depths to which the roots of a feeling reach in the soul of a solitary being thus returning to the traditions of mother-love in order to bestow upon a woman the same caressing devotion with which his mother had charmed his life? To him, what grandeur in these nothings wherein were blended his only two affections. Flowers and music thus became the language of their love. Gabrielle replied to Etienne's gifts by nosegays of her own, - nosegays which told the wise old doctor that his ignorant daughter already knew enough. The material ignorance of these two lovers was like a dark background on which the faintest lines of their all-spiritual intercourse were traced with exquisite delicacy, like the red, pure outlines of Etruscan figures. Their slightest words brought a flood of ideas, because each was the fruit of their long meditations. Incapable of boldly looking forward, each beginning seemed to them an end. Though absolutely free, they were imprisoned in their own simplicity, which would have been disheartening had either given a meaning to their confused desires. They were poets and poem both. Music, the most sensual of arts for loving souls, was the interpreter of their ideas; they took delight in repeating the same harmony, letting their passion flow through those fine sheets of sound in which their souls could vibrate without obstacle.

Many loves proceed through opposition; through struggles and reconciliations, the vulgar struggle of mind and matter. But the first wing-beat of true love sends it far beyond such struggles. Where all is of the same essence, two natures are no longer to be distinguished; like genius in its highest expression, such love can sustain itself in the brightest light; it grows beneath the light, it needs no shade to bring it into relief. Gabrielle, because she was a woman, Etienne, because he had suffered much and meditated much, passed quickly through the regions occupied by common passions and went beyond it. Like all enfeebled natures, they were quickly penetrated by Faith, by that celestial glow which doubles strength by doubling the soul. For them their sun was always at its meridian. Soon they had that divine belief in themselves which allows of neither jealousy nor torment; abnegation was ever ready, admiration constant.

Under these conditions, love could have no pain. Equal in their feebleness, strong in their union, if the noble had some superiority of knowledge and some conventional grandeur, the daughter of the physician eclipsed all that by her beauty, by the loftiness of her sentiments, by the delicacy she gave to their enjoyments. Thus these two white doves flew with one wing beneath their pure blue heaven; Etienne loved, he was loved, the present was serene, the future cloudless; he was sovereign lord; the castle was his, the sea belonged to both of them; no vexing thought troubled the harmonious concert of their canticle; virginity of mind and senses enlarged for them the world, their thoughts rose in their minds without effort; desire, the satisfactions of which are doomed to blast so much, desire, that evil of terrestrial love, had not as yet attacked them. Like two zephyrs swaying on the same willow-branch, they needed nothing more than the joy of looking at each other in the mirror of the limpid waters; immensity sufficed them; they admired their Ocean, without one thought of gliding on it in the white-winged bark with ropes of flowers, sailed by Hope.

Love has its moment when it suffices to itself, when it is happy in merely being. During this springtime, when all is budding, the lover sometimes hides from the beloved woman, in order to enjoy her more, to see her better; but Etienne and Gabrielle plunged together into all the delights of that infantine period. Sometimes they were two sisters in the grace of their confidences, sometimes two brothers in the boldness of their questionings. Usually love demands a slave and a god, but these two realized the dream of Plato, - they were but one being deified. They protected each other. Caresses came slowly, one by one, but chaste as the merry play - so graceful, so coquettish - of young animals. The sentiment which induced them to express their souls in song led them to love by the manifold transformations of the same happiness. Their joys caused them neither wakefulness nor delirium. It was the infancy of pleasure developing within them, unaware of the beautiful red flowers which were to crown its shoots. They gave themselves to each other, ignorant of all danger; they cast their whole being into a word, into a look, into a kiss, into the long, long pressure of their clasping hands. They praised each ther's beauties ingenuously, spending treasures of language on these secret idylls, inventing soft exaggerations and more diminutives than the ancient muse of Tibullus, or the poesies of Italy. On their lips and in their hearts love flowed ever, like the liquid fringes of the sea upon the sands of the shore, - all alike, all dissimilar. Joyous, eternal fidelity!

If we must count by days, the time thus spent was five months only; if we may count by the innumerable sensations, thoughts, dreams, glances, opening flowers, realized hopes, unceasing joys, speeches interrupted, renewed, abandoned, frolic laughter, bare feet dabbling in the sea, hunts, childlike, for shells, kisses, surprises, clasping hands, - call it a lifetime; death will justify the word. There are existences that are ever gloomy, lived under ashen skies; but suppose a glorious day, when the sun of heaven glows in the azure air, - such was the May of their love, during which Etienne had suspended all his griefs, - griefs which had passed into the heart of Gabrielle, who, in turn, had fastened all her joys to come on those of her lord. Etienne had had but one sorrow in his life, - the death of his mother; he was to have but one love - Gabrielle.

CHAPTER VII

THE CRUSHED PEARL

The coarse rivalry of an ambitious man hastened the destruction of this honeyed life. The Duc d'Herouville, an old warrior in wiles and policy, had no sooner passed his word to his physician than he was conscious of the voice of distrust. The Baron d'Artagnon, lieutenant of his company of men-at-arms, possessed his utmost confidence. The baron was a man after the duke's own heart, - a species of butcher, built for strength, tall, virile in face, cold and harsh, brave in the service of the throne, rude in his manners, with an iron will in action, but supple in manoeuvres, withal an ambitious noble, possessing the honor of a soldier and the wiles of a politician. He had the hand his face demanded, - large and hairy like that of a guerrilla; his manners were brusque, his speech concise. The duke, in departing, gave to this man the duty of watching and reporting to him the conduct of Beauvouloir toward the new heir-presumptive.

In spite of the secrecy which surrounded Gabrielle, it was difficult to long deceive the commander of a company. He heard the singing of two voices; he saw the lights at night in the dwelling on the seashore; he guessed that Etienne's orders, repeated constantly, for flowers concerned a woman; he discovered Gabrielle's

Honore de Balzac

nurse making her way on foot to Forcalier, carrying linen or clothes, and bringing back with her the work-frame and other articles needed by a young lady. The spy then watched the cottage, saw the physician's daughter, and fell in love with her. Beauvouloir he knew was rich. The duke would be furious at the man's audacity. On those foundations the Baron d'Artagnon erected the edifice of his fortunes. The duke, on learning that his son was falling in love, would, of course, instantly endeavor to detach him from the girl; what better way than to force her son into a marriage with a noble like himself, giving his son to the daughter of some great house, the heiress of large estates. The baron himself had no property. The scheme was excellent, and might have succeeded with other natures than those of Etienne and Gabrielle; with them failure was certain.

During his stay in Paris the duke had avenged the death of Maximilien by killing his son's adversary, and he had planned for Etienne an alliance with the heiress of a branch of the house of Grandlieu, - a tall and disdainful beauty, who was flattered by the prospect of some day bearing the title of Duchesse d'Herouville. The duke expected to oblige his son to marry her. On learning from d'Artagnon that Etienne was in love with the daughter of a miserable physician, he was only the more determined to carry out the marriage. What could such a man comprehend of love, - he who had let his own wife die beside him without understanding a single sigh of her heart? Never, perhaps, in his life had he felt such violent anger as when the last despatch of the baron told him with what rapidity Beauvouloir's plans were advancing, - the baron attributing them wholly to the bonesetter's ambition. The duke ordered out his equipages and started for Rouen, bringing with him the Comtesse de Grandlieu, her sister the Marquise de Noirmoutier, and Mademoiselle de Grandlieu, under pretext of showing them the province of Normandy.

A few days before his arrival a rumor was spread about the country - by what means no one seemed to know - of the passion of the young Duc de Nivron for Gabrielle Beauvouloir. People in Rouen spoke of it to the Duc d'Herouville in the midst of a banquet given to celebrate his return to the province; for the guests were glad to deliver a blow to the despot of Normandy. This announcement excited the anger of the governor to the highest pitch. He wrote to the baron to keep his coming to Herouville a close secret, giving him certain orders to avert what he considered to be an evil.

It was under these circumstances that Etienne and Gabrielle unrolled their thread through the labyrinth of love, where both, not seeking to leave it, thought to dwell. One day they had remained from morn to evening near the window where so many events had taken place. The hours, filled at first with gentle talk, had ended in meditative silence. They began to feel within them the wish for complete possession; and presently they reached the point of confiding to each other their confused ideas, the reflections of two beautiful, pure souls. During these still, serene hours, Etienne's eyes would sometimes fill with tears as he held the hand of Gabrielle to his lips. Like his mother, but at this moment happier in his love than she had been in hers, the hated son looked down upon the sea, at that hour golden on the shore, black on the horizon, and slashed here and there with those silvery caps which betoken a coming storm. Gabrielle, conforming to her friend's action, looked at the sight and was silent. A single look, one of those by which two souls support each other, sufficed to communicate their thoughts. Each loved with that love so divinely like unto itself at every instant of its eternity that it is not conscious of devotion or sacrifice or exaction, it fears neither deceptions nor delay. But Etienne and Gabrielle were in absolute ignorance of satisfactions, a desire for which was stirring in their souls.

When the first faint tints of twilight drew a veil athwart the sea, and the hush was interrupted only by the soughing of the flux and reflux on the shore, Etienne rose; Gabrielle followed his motion with a vague fear, for he had dropped her hand. He took her in one of his arms, pressing her to him with a movement of tender cohesion, and she, comprehending his desire, made him feel the weight of her body enough to give him the certainty that she was all his, but not enough to be a burden on him. The lover laid his head heavily on the shoulder of his friend, his lips touched the heaving bosom, his hair flowed over the white shoulders and caressed her throat. The girl, ingenuously loving, bent her head aside to give more place for his head, passing her arm about his neck to gain support. Thus they remained till nightfall without uttering a word. The crickets sang in their holes, and the lovers listened to that music as if to employ their senses on one sense only. Certainly they could only in that hour be compared to angels who, with their feet on earth, await the moment to take flight to heaven. They had fulfilled the noble dream of Plato's mystic genius, the dream of all who seek a meaning in humanity; they formed but one soul, they were, indeed, that mysterious Pearl destined to adorn the brow of a star as yet unknown, but the hope of all!

"Will you take me home?" said Gabrielle, the first to break the exquisite silence.

"Why should we part?" replied Etienne.

"We ought to be together always," she said.

"Stay with me."

"Yes."

The heavy step of Beauvouloir sounded in the adjoining room. The doctor had seen these children at the window locked in each other's arms, but he found them separated. The purest love demands its mystery.

"This is not right, my child," he said to Gabrielle, "to stay so late, and have no lights."

"Why wrong?" she said; "you know we love each other, and he is master of the castle."

"My children," said Beauvouloir, "if you love each other, your happiness requires that you should marry and pass your lives together; but your marriage depends on the will of monseigneur the duke -"

"My father has promised to gratify all my wishes," cried Etienne eagerly, interrupting Beauvouloir.

"Write to him, monseigneur," replied the doctor, and give me your letter that I may enclose it with one which I, myself, have just written. Bertrand is to start at once and put these despatches into monseigneur's own hand. I have learned to-night that he is now in Rouen; he has brought the heiress of the house of

Grandlieu with him, not, as I think, solely for himself. If I listened to my presentiments, I should take Gabrielle away from here this very night."

"Separate us?" cried Etienne, half fainting with distress and leaning on his love.

"Father!"

"Gabrielle," said the physician, holding out to her a smelling-bottle which he took from a table signing to her to make Etienne inhale its contents, - "Gabrielle, my knowledge of science tells me that Nature destined you for each other. I meant to prepare monseigneur the duke for a marriage which will certainly offend his ideas, but the devil has already prejudiced him against it. Etienne is Duc de Nivron, and you, my child, are the daughter of a poor doctor."

"My father swore to contradict me in nothing," said Etienne, calmly.

"He swore to me also to consent to all I might do in finding you a wife," replied the doctor; "but suppose that he does not keep his promises?"

Etienne sat down, as if overcome.

"The sea was dark to-night," he said, after a moment's silence.

"If you could ride a horse, monseigneur," said Beauvouloir, "I should tell you to fly with Gabrielle this very evening. I know you both, and I know that any other marriage would be fatal to you. The duke would certainly fling me into a dungeon and leave me there for the rest of my days when he heard of your flight; and I should die joyfully if my death secured your happiness. But alas! to mount a horse would risk your life and that of Gabrielle. We must face your father's anger here."

"Here!" repeated Etienne.

"We have been betrayed by some one in the chateau who has stirred your father's wrath against us," continued Beauvouloir.

"Let us throw ourselves together into the sea," said Etienne to Gabrielle, leaning down to the ear of the young girl who was kneeling beside him.

She bowed her head, smiling. Beauvouloir divined all.

"Monseigneur," he said, "your mind and your knowledge can make you eloquent, and the force of your love may be irresistible. Declare it to monseigneur the duke; you will thus confirm my letter. All is not lost, I think. I love my daughter as well as you love her, and I shall defend her."

Etienne shook his head.

"The sea was very dark to-night," he repeated.

"It was like a sheet of gold at our feet," said Gabrielle in a voice of melody.

Etienne ordered lights, and sat down at a table to write to his father. On one side of him knelt Gabrielle, silent, watching the words he wrote, but not reading them; she read all on Etienne's forehead. On his other side stood old Beauvouloir, whose jovial countenance was deeply sad, - sad as that gloomy chamber where Etienne's mother died. A secret voice cried to the doctor, "The fate of his mother awaits him!"

When the letter was written, Etienne held it out to the old man, who hastened to give it to Bertrand. The old retainer's horse was waiting in the courtyard, saddled; the man himself was ready. He started, and met the duke twelve miles from Herouville.

"Come with me to the gate of the courtyard," said Gabrielle to her friend when they were alone.

The pair passed through the cardinal's library, and went down through the tower, in which was a door, the key of which Etienne had given to Gabrielle. Stupefied by the dread of coming evil, the poor youth left in the tower the torch he had brought to light the steps of his beloved, and continued with her toward the cottage. A few steps from the little garden, which formed a sort of flowery courtyard to the humble habitation, the lovers stopped. Emboldened by the vague alarm which oppressed them, they gave each other, in the shades of night, in the silence, that first kiss in which the senses and the soul unite, and cause a revealing joy. Etienne comprehended love in its dual expression, and Gabrielle fled lest she should be drawn by that love - whither she knew not.

At the moment when the Duc de Nivron reascended the staircase to the castle, after closing the door of the tower, a cry of horror, uttered by Gabrielle, echoed in his ears with the sharpness of a flash of lightning which burns the eyes. Etienne ran through the apartments of the chateau, down the grand staircase, and along the beach towards Gabrielle's house, where he saw lights.

When Gabrielle, quitting her lover, had entered the little garden, she saw, by the gleam of a torch which lighted her nurse's spinning-wheel, the figure of a man sitting in the chair of that excellent woman. At the sound of her steps the man arose and came toward her; this had frightened her, and she gave the cry. The presence and aspect of the Baron d'Artagnon amply justified the fear thus inspired in the young girl's breast.

"Are you the daughter of Beauvouloir, monseigneur's physician?" asked the baron when Gabrielle's first alarm had subsided.

"Yes, monsieur."

"I have matters of the utmost importance to confide to you. I am the Baron d'Artagnon, lieutenant of the company of men-at-arms commanded by Monseigneur the Duc d'Herouville."

Gabrielle, under the circumstances in which she and her lover stood, was struck by these words, and by the frank tone with which the soldier said them.

"Your nurse is here; she may overhear us. Come this way," said the baron.

He left the garden, and Gabrielle followed him to the beach behind the house.

"Fear nothing!" said the baron.

That speech would have frightened any one less ignorant than Gabrielle; but a simple young girl who loves never thinks herself in peril.

"Dear child," said the baron, endeavoring to give a honeyed tone to his voice, "you and your father are on the verge of an abyss into which you will fall to-morrow. I cannot see your danger without warning you. Monseigneur is furious against your father and against you; he suspects you of having seduced his son, and he would rather see him dead than see him marry you; so much for his son. As for your father, this is the decision monseigneur has made about him. Nine years ago your father was implicated in a criminal affair. The matter related to the secretion of a child of rank at the time of its birth which he attended. Monseigneur, knowing that your father was innocent, guaranteed him from prosecution by the parliament; but now he intends to have him arrested and delivered up to justice to be tried for the crime. Your father will be broken on the wheel; though perhaps, in view of some services he has done to his master, he may obtain the favor of being hanged. I do not know what course monseigneur has decided on for you; but I do know that you can save Monseigneur de Nivron from his father's anger, and your father from the horrible death which awaits him, and also save yourself."

"What must I do?" said Gabrielle.

"Throw yourself at monseigneur's feet, and tell him that his son loves you against your will, and say that you do not love him. In proof of this, offer to marry any man whom the duke himself may select as your husband. He is generous; he will dower you handsomely."

"I can do all except deny my love."

"But if that alone can save your father, yourself, and Monseigneur de Nivron?"

"Etienne," she replied, "would die of it, and so should I."

"Monseigneur de Nivron will be unhappy at losing you, but he will live for the honor of his house; you will resign yourself to be the wife of a baron only, instead of being a duchess, and your father will live out his days," said the practical man.

At this moment Etienne reached the house. He did not see Gabrielle, and he uttered a piercing cry.

"He is here!" cried the young girl; "let me go now and comfort him."

"I shall come for your answer to-morrow," said the baron.

"I will consult my father," she replied.

"You will not see him again. I have received orders to arrest him and send him in chains, under escort, to Rouen," said d'Artagnon, leaving Gabrielle dumb with terror.

The young girl sprang to the house, and found Etienne horrified by the silence of the nurse in answer to his question, "Where is she?"

"I am here!" cried the young girl, whose voice was icy, her step heavy, her color gone.

"What has happened?" he said. "I heard you cry."

"Yes, I hurt my foot against -"

"No, love," replied Etienne, interrupting her. "I heard the steps of a man."

"Etienne, we must have offended God; let us kneel down and pray. I will tell you afterwards."

Etienne and Gabrielle knelt down at the prie-dieu, and the nurse recited her rosary.

"O God!" prayed the girl, with a fervor which carried her beyond terrestrial space, "if we have not sinned against thy divine commandments, if we have not offended the Church, not yet the king, we, who are one and the same being, in whom love shines with the light that thou hast given to the pearl of the sea, be merciful unto us, and let us not be parted either in this world or in that which is to come."

"Mother!" added Etienne, "who art in heaven, obtain from the Virgin that if we cannot - Gabrielle and I - be happy here below we may at least die together, and without suffering. Call us, and we will go to thee."

Then, having recited their evening prayers, Gabrielle related her interview with Baron d'Artagnon.

"Gabrielle," said the young man, gathering strength from his despair, "I shall know how to resist my father."

He kissed her on the forehead, but not again upon the lips. Then he returned to the castle, resolved to face the terrible man who had weighed so fearfully on his life.

He did not know that Gabrielle's house would be surrounded and guarded by soldiers the moment that he quitted it.

The next day he was struck down with grief when, on going to see her, he found her a prisoner. But Gabrielle sent her nurse to tell him she would die sooner than be false to him; and, moreover, that she knew a way to deceive the guards, and would soon take refuge in the cardinal's library, where no one would suspect her presence, though she did not as yet know when she could accomplish it. Etienne on that returned to his room, where all the forces of his heart were spent in the dreadful suspense of waiting.

At three o'clock on the afternoon of that day the equipages of the duke and suite entered the courtyard of the castle. Madame la Comtesse de Grandlieu, leaning on the arm of her daughter, the duke and Marquise de Noirmoutier mounted the grand staircase in silence, for the stern brow of the master had awed the servants. Though Baron d'Artagnon now knew that Gabrielle had evaded his guards, he assured the duke she was a prisoner, for he trembled lest his own private scheme should fail if the duke were angered by this flight. Those two terrible faces - his and the duke's - wore a fierce expression that was ill-disguised by an air of gallantry imposed by the occasion. The duke had already sent to his son, ordering him to be present in the salon. When the company entered it, d'Artagnon saw by the downcast look on Etienne's face that as yet he did not know of Gabrielle's escape.

"This is my son," said the old duke, taking Etienne by the hand and presenting him to the ladies.

Etienne bowed without uttering a word. The countess and Mademoiselle de Grandlieu exchanged a look which the old man intercepted.

"Your daughter will be ill-matched - is that your thought?" he said in a low voice.

"I think quite the contrary, my dear duke," replied the mother, smiling.

The Marquise de Noirmoutier, who accompanied her sister, laughed significantly. That laugh stabbed Etienne to the heart; already the sight of the tall lady had terrified him.

"Well, Monsieur le duc," said the duke in a low voice and assuming a lively air, "have I not found you a handsome wife? What do you say to that slip of a girl, my cherub?"

The old duke never doubted his son's obedience; Etienne, to him, was the son of his mother, of the same dough, docile to his kneading.

"Let him have a child and die," thought the old man; "little I care."

"Father," said the young man, in a gentle voice, "I do not understand you."

"Come into your own room, I have a few words to say to you," replied the duke, leading the way into the state bedroom.

Etienne followed his father. The three ladies, stirred with a curiosity that was shared by Baron d'Artagnon, walked about the great salon in a manner to group themselves finally near the door of the bedroom, which the duke had left partially open.

"Dear Benjamin," said the duke, softening his voice, "I have selected that tall and handsome young lady as your wife; she is heiress to the estates of the younger branch of the house of Grandlieu, a fine old family of Bretagne. Therefore make yourself agreeable; reme-mber all the love-making you have read of in your books, and learn to make pretty speeches."

"Father, is it not the first duty of a nobleman to keep his word?"

"Yes."

"Well, then, on the day when I forgave you the death of my mother, dying here through her marriage with you, did you not promise me never to thwart my wishes? 'I will obey you as the family god,' were the words you said to me. I ask nothing of you, I simply demand my freedom in a matter which concerns my life and myself only, - namely, my marriage."

"I understood," replied the old man, all the blood in his body rushing into his face, "that you would not oppose the continuation of our noble race."

"You made no condition," said Etienne. "I do not know what love has to do with race; but this I know, I love the daughter of your old friend Beauvouloir, and the granddaughter of your friend La Belle Romaine."

"She is dead," replied the old colossus, with an air both

Honore de Balzac

savage and jeering, which told only too plainly his intention of making away with her.

A moment of deep silence followed.

The duke saw, through the half-opened door, the three ladies and d'Artagnon. At that crucial moment Etienne, whose sense of hearing was acute, heard in the cardinal's library poor Gabrielle's voice, singing, to let her lover know she was there, -

"Ermine hath not
Her pureness;
The lily not her whiteness."

The hated son, whom his father's horrible speech had flung into a gulf of death, returned to the surface of life at the sound of that voice. Though the emotion of terror thus rapidly cast off had already in that instant, broken his heart, he gathered up his strength, looked his father in the face for the first time in his life, gave scorn for scorn, and said, in tones of hatred: -

"A nobleman ought not to lie."

Then with one bound he sprang to the door of the library and cried: -

"Gabrielle!"

Suddenly the gentle creature appeared among the shadows, like the lily among its leaves, trembling before those mocking women thus informed of Etienne's love. As the clouds that bear the thunder project upon the heavens, so the old duke, reaching a degree of anger that defies description, stood out upon the brilliant background produced by the rich clothing of those courtly dames. Between the destruction of his son and a mesalliance, every other father would have hesitated, but in this uncontrollable old man ferocity was the power which had so far solved the difficulties of life for him; he drew his sword in all cases, as the only remedy that he knew for the gordian knots of life. Under present circumstances, when the convulsion of his ideas had reached its height, the nature of the man came uppermost. Twice detected in flagrant falsehood by the being he abhorred, the son he cursed, cursing him more than ever in this supreme moment when that son's despised, and to him most despicable, weakness triumphed over his own omnipotence, infallible till then, the father and the man ceased to exist, the tiger issued from its lair. Casting at the angels before him - the sweetest pair that ever set their feet on earth - a murderous look of hatred, -

"Die, then, both of you!" he cried. "You, vile abortion, the proof of my shame - and you," he said to Gabrielle, "miserable strumpet with the viper tongue, who has poisoned my house."

These words struck home to the hearts of the two children the terror that already surcharged them. At the moment when Etienne saw the huge hand of his father raising a weapon upon Gabrielle he died, and Gabrielle fell dead in striving to retain him.

The old man left them, and closed the door violently, saying to Mademoiselle de Grandlieu: -

"I will marry you myself!"

"You are young and gallant enough to have a fine new

lineage," whispered the countess in the ear of the old man, who had served under seven kings of France.

Choose from Thousands of 1stWorldLibrary Classics By

A. M. Barnard	C. M. Ingleby	Elizabeth Gaskell
Ada Leverson	Carolyn Wells	Elizabeth McCracken
Adolphus William Ward	Catherine Parr Traill	Elizabeth Von Arnim
Aesop	Charles A. Eastman	Ellem Key
Agatha Christie	Charles Amory Beach	Emerson Hough
Alexander Aaronsohn	Charles Dickens	Emilie F. Carlen
Alexander Kielland	Charles Dudley Warner	Emily Dickinson
Alexandre Dumas	Charles Farrar Browne	Enid Bagnold
Alfred Gatty	Charles Ives	Enilor Macartney Lane
Alfred Ollivant	Charles Kingsley	Erasmus W. Jones
Alice Duer Miller	Charles Klein	Ernie Howard Pie
Alice Turner Curtis	Charles Hanson Towne	Ethel May Dell
Alice Dunbar	Charles Lathrop Pack	Ethel Turner
Allen Chapman	Charles Romyn Dake	Ethel Watts Mumford
Ambrose Bierce	Charles Whibley	Eugenie Foa
Amelia E. Barr	Charles Willing Beale	Eugene Wood
Amory H. Bradford	Charlotte M. Braeme	Eustace Hale Ball
Andrew Lang	Charlotte M. Yonge	Evelyn Everett-green
Andrew McFarland Davis	Charlotte Perkins Stetson	Everard Cotes
Andy Adams	Clair W. Hayes	F. H. Cheley
Anna Alice Chapin	Clarence Day Jr.	F. J. Cross
Anna Sewell	Clarence E. Mulford	F. Marion Crawford
Annie Besant	Clemence Housman	Federick Austin Ogg
Annie Hamilton Donnell	Confucius	Ferdinand Ossendowski
Annie Payson Call	Coningsby Dawson	Francis Bacon
Annie Roe Carr	Cornelis DeWitt Wilcox	Francis Darwin
Annonaymous	Cyril Burleigh	Frances Hodgson Burnett
Anton Chekhov	D. H. Lawrence	Frances Parkinson Keyes
Arnold Bennett	Daniel Defoe	Frank Gee Patchin
Arthur Conan Doyle	David Garnett	Frank Harris
Arthur M. Winfield	Dinah Craik	Frank Jewett Mather
Arthur Ransome	Don Carlos Janes	Frank L. Packard
Arthur Schnitzler	Donald Keyhoe	Frank V. Webster
Atticus	Dorothy Kilner	Frederic Stewart Isham
B.H. Baden-Powell	Dougan Clark	Frederick Trevor Hill
B. M. Bower	Douglas Fairbanks	Frederick Winslow Taylor
B. C. Chatterjee	E. Nesbit	Friedrich Kerst
Baroness Emmuska Orczy	E.P.Roe	Friedrich Nietzsche
Baroness Orczy	E. Phillips Oppenheim	Fyodor Dostoyevsky
Basil King	Earl Barnes	G.A. Henty
Bayard Taylor	Edgar Rice Burroughs	G.K. Chesterton
Ben Macomber	Edith Van Dyne	Gabrielle E. Jackson
Bertha Muzzy Bower	Edith Wharton	Garrett P. Serviss
Bjornstjerne Bjornson	Edward Everett Hale	Gaston Leroux
Booth Tarkington	Edward J. O'Biren	George A. Warren
Boyd Cable	Edward S. Ellis	George Ade
Bram Stoker	Edwin L. Arnold	Geroge Bernard Shaw
C. Collodi	Eleanor Atkins	George Durston
C. E. Orr	Eliot Gregory	George Ebers

George Eliot
George Gissing
George MacDonald
George Meredith
George Orwell
George Sylvester Viereck
George Tucker
George W. Cable
George Wharton James
Gertrude Atherton
Gordon Casserly
Grace E. King
Grace Gallatin
Grace Greenwood
Grant Allen
Guillermo A. Sherwell
Gulielma Zollinger
Gustav Flaubert
H. A. Cody
H. B. Irving
H.C. Bailey
H. G. Wells
H. H. Munro
H. Irving Hancock
H. Rider Haggard
H. W. C. Davis
Haldeman Julius
Hall Caine
Hamilton Wright Mabie
Hans Christian Andersen
Harold Avery
Harold McGrath
Harriet Beecher Stowe
Harry Castlemon
Harry Coghill
Harry Houidini
Hayden Carruth
Helent Hunt Jackson
Helen Nicolay
Hendrik Conscience
Hendy David Thoreau
Henri Barbusse
Henrik Ibsen
Henry Adams
Henry Ford
Henry Frost
Henry James
Henry Jones Ford
Henry Seton Merriman
Henry W Longfellow
Herbert A. Giles

Herbert Carter
Herbert N. Casson
Herman Hesse
Hildegard G. Frey
Homer
Honore De Balzac
Horace B. Day
Horace Walpole
Horatio Alger Jr.
Howard Pyle
Howard R. Garis
Hugh Lofting
Hugh Walpole
Humphry Ward
Ian Maclaren
Inez Haynes Gillmore
Irving Bacheller
Isabel Hornibrook
Israel Abrahams
Ivan Turgenev
J.G.Austin
J. Henri Fabre
J. M. Barrie
J. Macdonald Oxley
J. S. Fletcher
J. S. Knowles
J. Storer Clouston
Jack London
Jacob Abbott
James Allen
James Andrews
James Baldwin
James Branch Cabell
James DeMille
James Joyce
James Lane Allen
James Lane Allen
James Oliver Curwood
James Oppenheim
James Otis
James R. Driscoll
Jane Austen
Jane L. Stewart
Janet Aldridge
Jens Peter Jacobsen
Jerome K. Jerome
John Burroughs
John Cournos
John F. Kennedy
John Gay
John Glasworthy

John Habberton
John Joy Bell
John Kendrick Bangs
John Milton
John Philip Sousa
Jonas Lauritz Idemil Lie
Jonathan Swift
Joseph A. Altsheler
Joseph Carey
Joseph Conrad
Joseph E. Badger Jr
Joseph Hergesheimer
Joseph Jacobs
Jules Vernes
Julian Hawthrone
Julie A Lippmann
Justin Huntly McCarthy
Kakuzo Okakura
Kenneth Grahame
Kenneth McGaffey
Kate Langley Bosher
Kate Langley Bosher
Katherine Cecil Thurston
Katherine Stokes
L. A. Abbot
L. T. Meade
L. Frank Baum
Latta Griswold
Laura Dent Crane
Laura Lee Hope
Laurence Housman
Lawrence Beasley
Leo Tolstoy
Leonid Andreyev
Lewis Carroll
Lewis Sperry Chafer
Lilian Bell
Lloyd Osbourne
Louis Hughes
Louis Tracy
Louisa May Alcott
Lucy Fitch Perkins
Lucy Maud Montgomery
Luther Benson
Lydia Miller Middleton
Lyndon Orr
M. Corvus
M. H. Adams
Margaret E. Sangster
Margret Howth
Margaret Vandercook

Margret Penrose
Maria Edgeworth
Maria Thompson Daviess
Mariano Azuela
Marion Polk Angellotti
Mark Overton
Mark Twain
Mary Austin
Mary Catherine Crowley
Mary Cole
Mary Hastings Bradley
Mary Roberts Rinehart
Mary Rowlandson
M. Wollstonecraft Shelley
Maud Lindsay
Max Beerbohm
Myra Kelly
Nathaniel Hawthrone
Nicolo Machiavelli
O. F. Walton
Oscar Wilde
Owen Johnson
P.G. Wodehouse
Paul and Mabel Thorne
Paul G. Tomlinson
Paul Severing
Percy Brebner
Peter B. Kyne
Plato
R. Derby Holmes
R. L. Stevenson
R. S. Ball
Rabindranath Tagore
Rahul Alvares
Ralph Bonehill
Ralph Henry Barbour
Ralph Victor
Ralph Waldo Emmerson
Rene Descartes
Rex Beach

Rex E. Beach
Richard Harding Davis
Richard Jefferies
Richard Le Gallienne
Robert Barr
Robert Frost
Robert Gordon Anderson
Robert L. Drake
Robert Lansing
Robert Lynd
Robert Michael Ballantyne
Robert W. Chambers
Rosa Nouchette Carey
Rudyard Kipling
Samuel B. Allison
Samuel Hopkins Adams
Sarah Bernhardt
Sarah C. Hallowell
Selma Lagerlof
Sherwood Anderson
Sigmund Freud
Standish O'Grady
Stanley Weyman
Stella Benson
Stella M. Francis
Stephen Crane
Stewart Edward White
Stijn Streuvels
Swami Abhedananda
Swami Parmananda
T. S. Ackland
T. S. Arthur
The Princess Der Ling
Thomas A. Janvier
Thomas A Kempis
Thomas Anderton
Thomas Bailey Aldrich
Thomas Bulfinch
Thomas De Quincey
Thomas Dixon

Thomas H. Huxley
Thomas Hardy
Thomas More
Thornton W. Burgess
U. S. Grant
Valentine Williams
Various Authors
Vaughan Kester
Victor Appleton
Victoria Cross
Virginia Woolf
Wadsworth Camp
Walter Camp
Walter Scott
Washington Irving
Wilbur Lawton
Wilkie Collins
Willa Cather
Willard F. Baker
William Dean Howells
William le Queux
W. Makepeace Thackeray
William W. Walter
William Shakespeare
Winston Churchill
Yei Theodora Ozaki
Yogi Ramacharaka
Young E. Allison
Zane Grey

www.ingramcontent.com/pod-product-compliance
Lightning Source LLC
Chambersburg PA
CBHW020505100426
42813CB00030B/3128/J